"Jane Turner is all guts and compassion. And you want that in a coach. She has this incredible capacity for deep, genuine empathy bundled up with the wisdom of 'one who has gone before'. I've always walked away from conversations with her teeming with new insights about myself, and how I engage with the world — she's absolutely top-shelf stuff!"
Alicia Cook - Coach and Consultant, Havingcake.com

"Jane has a very calming, relaxing personality and coaching style. You feel her openness, and interest in what you are exploring, which helps to unlock with ease many layers of your being while feeling safe and supported."
Maja Skrlg Tufegdzic - Transpersonal Coach

"Having a coach like Jane gives me the inside running. I'm now writing better, performing well, losing weight and facing the future with enough"
"wisdom to avoid the old tricks of mind, body and spirit."
David O'Brien - Playwright, Actor, Scriptwriter, Journalist and Film Maker

"Jane has made an incredible impact on my life. Her warmth and sincerity was a comfort whilst I searched for inner guidance. Once I found this, her wise words, positivity and support helped me to facilitate the change I was seeking — thank you Jane for being there for me every step of the way"
Bree Shearer - Studio Manager

"From the minute I sat down with Jane I felt relaxed, at ease and able to just be Me. She has a warm, grounding energy about her. Immediately I noticed her beautiful rich deep speaking voice; it was calming and welcoming and it settled my mind. I remember thinking to myself, "This woman knows who she is. She has a backstory. And she'll be cool with whatever I have to say." She just felt REAL to me. I always feel safe and supported when I talk to Jane. Not only is she intuitive, stimulating and observant as a coach, but also, she invites reflection and allows time for musing/pondering. I get the impression that Jane's life has been a series of deep learning experiences, and she inspires others to view their journey in the same way. Her supportive presence has made a wonderful impact on my life."
Shana Quinn - Transpersonal Coach

WEIGHT LOSS IN MIDLIFE

How to get out of the diet trap

Jane Turner

Copyright © 2017
All rights reserved. This book or any portion thereof may not be reproduced or used in any manner whatsoever without the express written permission of the author except for the use of brief quotations in a book review.

Printed in Australia
First Printing, 2017
ISBN: 978-0-6480026-7-3

White Light Publishing House
6 Lincoln Way
Melton West, VIC, Australia 3337
www.whitelightpublishing.com.au

Foreword

The first time I met Jane was sixty seconds before we stepped onto live TV. Camera crews in our face, producers with their clipboards, make-up girls dusting us and sound guys threading microphones through our bras. It's not what I would call an ideal setting to talk about one's personal struggle with weight. Yet that is what we were here to do, in front of these people. In front of the nation. You see Jane had been trialling a new diet for a morning show, and I was the nutritionist working with her. I had gotten to know a lot about Jane in the prior month via email, and I became fascinated by her story (as I know you will too). It struck me as we chatted that morning how relaxed, grounded and open Jane was. Anyone else would be shaking in their boots about to step on air! Jane has an inner strength that comes from experience, from the wisdom of learning, and from true self-belief. This woman knows her stuff and knows how to communicate it well.

Weight Loss In Midlife is a culmination of Jane's life lessons wrapped into seven chapters or 'Factors' that affect weight loss in midlife. From the Body Factor, to the Food, Mindset and Stress Factor, she tackles the biggest issues that hold us back from achieving a healthy weight. Her research, combined with experience and empathy provides such a rich learning opportunity for anyone struggling with their weight through midlife. There's no doubt Jane 'gets it.' She gets us - women, and our struggles with weight.

I've been in the weight loss industry for 20 years. I'm the co-founder of Australia's largest online weight loss business (Michelle Bridges 12WBT) and I have reviewed hundreds of diets over the years. I've seen it all! What I love about Jane's approach is that the chapters have simple yet effective practical tools you can use, which gets you actively involved instead of just passively reading. For example, in Chapter 4; The Mindset Factor there is a great flush out exercise, and self-compassion repair kit. In Chapter 6; The Stress Factor, the mind de-cluttering exercise is really effective. You may even want to jump to the factor that is your biggest bug bear, and tackle that one first. Maybe you can give yourself two weeks to master each factor before moving onto the next. I've LOVED getting to know Jane and I know you will too. Her approach is balanced, sensible, and effective. Connect with her story, be supported by her research, and most of all enjoy the physical and emotional evolution you are about to make. Happy reading!

Amelia Phillips
Health & Fitness Expert

Contents

	Page
Introduction	9
CHAPTER ONE – The Experience Factor	13
CHAPTER TWO – The Body Factor	29
CHAPTER THREE – The Food Factor	43
CHAPTER FOUR – The Mindset Factor	65
CHAPTER FIVE – The Sleep Factor	95
CHAPTER SIX – The Stress Factor	103
CHAPTER SEVEN – The Exercise Factor	129
Conclusion	141

Introduction

I wrote my first book *Thrive in Midlife* at the end of 2014. In it I shared the results of a range of lifestyle changes I put in place to deal with the onset of menopause. The bottom line is that focusing on what I was putting into my mouth, managing the level of stress I was exposed to, and introducing a gentle exercise regime, left me feeling a whole lot better than I'd felt for a very long time. Fast forward to today, and I'm living proof of the fact that results like these will dissipate if you take your hands off the wheel and slip back into patterns that don't serve you well. For someone like me with a long track record of messing around with my diet in particular, I can now see that a higher degree of commitment and focus than I applied through 2015 and most of 2016, is going to be key to maintaining good health and making sure that I don't fall back into bad habits as I move through midlife and beyond.

I'm not talking about working harder to stick to good habits, because anything that's going to wear you out will fail you in the end. What I'm talking about is getting clear about what's likely to emerge to make it hard for you to get started on the road to a healthier life in the first place, and/or what's going to make it difficult to sustain once the honeymoon period is over. I then offer you strategies to overcome things like self-sabotage and other mindset related potholes on the road to success. Just to be clear about this from the get-go, the success I'm talking about here is not a quick fix, but rather a holistic approach to wellbeing that comes in the form of establishing patterns that take you to your ideal weight and settle you in there for the long haul in an easeful and sustainable way.

This book is all about helping you to put solid foundations in place to manage your weight and predispose your body to age more slowly than it otherwise would, by helping you to understand the conditions your body needs to be well. This matters because carrying around extra kilos can lead to serious problems like high blood pressure, diabetes, heart disease and stroke.

As you work your way through this book you'll build up a very clear picture of where you're at right now, where you want to get to, what might prevent you from getting there, and how to get over any barriers that emerge in the process of making the changes you need to make to start working toward your health goals. Please don't skip over the chapter on mindset whatever you do. It's very clear to me now that mindset management is one of the fundamental strategies that is missing in the plethora of weight loss programs out there, and there's no doubt that the absence of this kind of foundational work is one of the things that contributes to the appalling statistic you've probably heard about: the fact that only 3% of the people who lose weight manage to keep it off for 12 months or more.

The mindset and other chapters focusing on the importance of things like managing your stress, and making sure that you get enough sleep, are all about taking a holistic approach to supporting you on your weight loss journey so that you manage to be in the minority group that gets to the weight they want to get to and manages to stay there. As you'll see in the mindset chapter, I consider this to be a Hero's Journey, and as such it's not to be underestimated. If you're not familiar with the Hero's Journey that was made famous by Joseph Campbell in his book *The Hero with a Thousand Faces*, I think you're going to gain a lot from applying this perspective to your struggle to maintain a healthy weight, because it will help you to see that your past does not dictate your future, and that through this book you now have the tools and support you need to get to your ideal weight and stay there.

My aim is to help you to overcome any resistance that might come up for you as you change your relationship with food and your body. I've taken this approach because I know from personal experience how strong the resistance can be. I also know how incredibly high the stakes are in terms of what you have to gain if you resist the resistance, and how much you have to lose if you don't.

More power to you for reaching out and arming yourself with a book like this. Your reward for doing so is to have me by your side the whole way. I invite you to visit me at www.wellnesscoachingcollective.com if there's ever anything you need in the way of external support from someone who has gone before you. I want nothing more than to see you achieve the results you're after in terms of setting yourself up for a happy and healthy future. Helping people like you to get out of the diet trap is what drives me these days.

What the diet industry doesn't want you to know is that there are a number of basic things you already have in your control to manage your weight, that have nothing to do with potions and pills, or powders and programs, that people wind up spending a fortune on that simply don't work in the long term, and probably won't work in the short term either if you don't look after the basics of getting a good night's sleep, managing your mindset so that you don't sabotage your efforts to get healthy, and managing your stress so that your body isn't operating in survival mode where it's focus is on storing fat rather than shedding it. The cold hard truth is that there is a lot of money tied up in recruiting people like you into an environment that's essentially a revolving door. Sadly, the fact is that solving your problem in the long term is counterproductive from the point of view of the companies whose profits are tied up in your ongoing patronage.

I'll leave you to ponder what I've just said, and to think about the quote from Albert Einstein below in light of the fact that you're now in a good position to decide that the world is not a hostile place, because you have all of the support you need to get to where you want to be.

The biggest decision you'll ever have to make is whether you live in a hostile world or not!

Albert Einstein

CHAPTER ONE

The Experience Factor

I'm now 54 and run a business called the Wellness Coaching Collective. This company incorporates a writing program that I designed to help other people just like me to get their books written. This program grew out of the incredibly cathartic experience I had when I wrote my first book *Thrive in Midlife* in 2014. The deep level of healing involved in writing my story down was something that I really didn't see coming, and I thank the heavens for the fact that it happened. I now love the fact that my experience can help others to get their books written so that they get to enjoy the kind of personal empowerment and business growth that becoming a published author achieved for me.

One of the unexpected consequences of writing my story down was that I experienced two incredibly powerful pieces of healing in the process. One of these came about as I was considering the options I had for handling menopause in 2014, compared with the options that my mother had when she was in the same position in the early 1980s. The stark reality here was that in my Mother's Day, synthetic hormones were prescribed without a second thought, and sadly she was one of the many women who paid the price in terms of being diagnosed with breast cancer in her late 60s.

I'm grateful to Tamoxifen which is still the drug of choice for treating breast cancer, because it bought my mother some extra time that gave her a chance to get to know my daughter Lucy. And it also gave Lucy a chance to get to know her grandmother. It was an all too brief, but lovely and important year that they each had to get to know each other.

I share this part of my story with you here because I literally felt my heart split open when I wrote about this beautiful relationship between my mother and my daughter. This was a huge deal for me because there were a couple of traumas around my entry into the world that fundamentally shaped the way I experienced my emotions right up to the time when I stumbled on tools like Neuro Linguistic Programming (NLP) that helped me to work through some of the baggage I'd accumulated over time. I was aware of one of these traumas, but the other one came as a complete shock to me. The one I was aware of had to do with the fact that my mother almost died from a blood clot that travelled to her lung just after giving birth to me. Meanwhile the bigger piece of the puzzle that I had no inkling of whatsoever relates to the fact that I was the surviving twin in a case of Vanishing Twin Syndrome. This didn't come to light until I was 45 and training to be a NLP Master Practitioner myself so that I could help other people to uncover and transcend any limiting beliefs that were holding them back. In fact, my awareness around the fact that I'd internalised the trauma of losing my twin in utero came about when I was helping the trainer to demonstrate Time Line Therapy. Time Line Therapy is a very powerful process used in NLP. Its effectiveness comes from the fact that it helps people to access material that's stored deep in the unconscious part of their mind.

As the name suggests, Vanishing Twin Syndrome comes about when a twin disappears in the uterus during pregnancy. Most mothers don't even know that this has happened because the foetal tissue is either absorbed by the other twin, or into the placenta. So, if this happens before an ultrasound has been done, there's no evidence whatsoever that the twin ever existed. What this means is that I could have gone through my whole life without finding out what caused the gnawing feeling of emptiness that I'd been harbouring deep inside of myself. One of the consequences of this is that before I was even born I learnt how to shut my feelings off to avoid the pain of abandonment that I felt in the first instance when my twin left me, and then again when my mother was absent in the early weeks of my life because she was teetering on the brink of death herself.

The problem with shutting your feelings off is that you can't just block the bad ones out. It's an all or nothing proposition. What this means is that our ability to feel emotions like joy, love, and bliss is compromised when we numb ourselves in order to avoid feeling the painful emotions like fear, grief, and sadness.

Looking back on all of this now, I feel sad when I think about spending so much of my life in an emotionally numb state. I also feel intensely sad about the fact that my mother and I never really got around to bonding properly while she was alive. But I have to say that I'm incredibly grateful for finally making up for that in the process of writing my first book some 10 years after she passed away. Among other things, what that experience of essentially reconnecting with my mother did was loosen the grip of the toxic relationship with food that I'd developed as a numbing strategy from a very young age.

This was a fantastic result in and of itself, but even better still was the fact that the universe stepped up to the mark at the end of 2014 by opening up a spot for me in clinical trials that were being run by Sydney University to gauge the efficacy of Eye Movement Desensitisation Reprocessing (EMDR) in the treatment of binge eating disorder. Some would say the fact that this happened two days after the cathartic experience I had in relation to posthumously bonding with my mother was a coincidence, but I think not. What I take it to mean was that I was finally ready to start the healing around this part of my life. This was a blessing I continue to be incredibly grateful for.

I'm all about giving back now, and in addition to being passionate about helping people to go on the journey of becoming an author, there will always be a special place in my heart for people who struggle with food. What I want to say upfront is that I know from first-hand experience that processed foods with flavour enhancers, high sugar content, or high salt content are addictive. It's as simple as that. Of course, you don't have to be dealing with food addiction to benefit from focussing on limiting toxic food from your life, but in particular if you are struggling with food addiction of any kind, you'll find that the level of awareness you get from reading this book and working your way through the mindset strategies in it, will help you get to a state where you can start to build the bridge back to a healthy relationship with food.

The changes I made in relation to mindset and stress management as part of my *Thrive in Midlife* project back in 2014 got me to a place where I'm finally able to own my story, and love the skin that I'm in no matter what weight I am, or how messy my past has been. This is a very powerful place to be in. Sure, this book is about weight loss, but losing weight is no longer the be-all and end-all for me, and I want to suggest that you'll also benefit from working on your perspective if you're one of the many people for whom somewhere along the track the matter of what you ate and did not eat started taking up way too much of your emotional energy. These days it's all about getting my body to an optimal state where it can function at its best. And this is what I'm here to help you to achieve as well. The irony is that it was only when I took the pressure off myself, and found a way of eating that really suited me, that I finally got down to and settled at a really healthy weight.

Needless to say, it's been a pretty circuitous journey to get to where I am right now. And I'll share a bit more of my background with you here before we get down to brass tacks and turn the focus on you. I do this because I want you to see that if I have been able to arrive at a place of freedom around food even with my incredibly screwed-up background around it, then so can you.

So, it all started back in 1962 when I was born into a family in middle-class Australia with a mum, a dad and four other kids. I had a fairly unexceptional life right up until 2001 when my beautiful daughter Lucy came into the world. Whilst motherhood was not a role that I was particularly well prepared for, or for that matter suited to at the time, the healing I was ultimately blessed with after being pushed way out of my comfort zone by motherhood was the thin end of the wedge of the personal development work I wound up doing prior to finally stepping up and owning my story warts and all, with the release of my book *Thrive in Midlife*.

The comfort zone that I mention above was one of entrenched denial wrapped around blissful ignorance about the harm I was doing to my body and my mind, with the toxic thought patterns and behaviours I'd developed decades earlier around my body image, and consequently around food. Those behaviours meant that by the time I became a mother just short of my 40th birthday, I had already laid down the foundations for the kind of chronic illness and painful decline that we commonly associate with ageing. Cancer, cardiovascular disease, obesity, type 2 diabetes, and dementia are the kinds of things I'm talking about here. None of these things are inevitable of course. But in retrospect I can see that I need to accept complete responsibility for the fact that I'd been tipping the scales in the wrong direction for a very long time before the state of my emotions, my mind, and my body started to cave in completely with the demands of becoming a new mother added on top of everything else.

The early years of the 21st century after the birth of my daughter were turbulent to say the very least. Under the shadow of depression in my mid-40s I started dabbling in healing modalities like NLP, Rebirthing, and more conventional modalities like Cognitive Behaviour Therapy and counselling. Then in 2007 I trained to become an NLP Master Practitioner and Behavioural Coach myself. Needless to say, taking part in this kind of training changed my life completely.

Thrive in Midlife was motivated by the reality check I had at the age of 52 when I started to descend into a really deep depression brought on by sleep deprivation and the skewed hormones that came along with the onset of menopause. Menopause is not a one-size-fits-all scenario of course, and in my own case it hit me like a freight train. In addition to sleep deprivation and depression, my experience included aching joints, mood swings, difficulty thinking straight, and night sweats. In short, my initial experience of menopause was unbearable, and that was what got me on the path of urgently finding out what conditions my body needed to be well in general, and what conditions it needed to be well during midlife in particular.

Fast forward two years to today, and I was given the opportunity to see whether a new approach to losing weight and aging well could help me to turn around the results of having slackened off in relation to the changes I made to my diet and exercise regimes when I wrote *Thrive in Midlife*. The upshot of it is that I wrote this book to share the wonderful results I ultimately achieved by incorporating Sirtfoods into my diet.
The Sirtfood approach is the brainchild of Aidan Goggins and Glen Matten who wrote a book called *The Health Delusion*. This approach is all about activating our sirtuin genes that are known to switch on fat-

burning and other natural anti-ageing mechanisms such as cellular detoxification. This trial came along at a perfect time for me because my clothes were starting to feel tight, and my body was starting to feel worn-out like it did when menopause first hit me a couple of years ago. Being involved in a trial like this with a high level of accountability was exactly what I needed, because I was wary of the possibility of falling into a trap I'd fallen into many times in the past. This trap involves a curious mental tick that kicked in more or less regularly in the bad old days when I would start diet after diet in an attempt to morph my body into the narrowly defined shape of feminine perfection that I was brought up with.

My gut feel is that this mental tick, or at least some version of it, will resonate with a lot of you, because people I interviewed for this book and for *Thrive in Midlife* who consider themselves to be very rational and sensible in almost every other aspect of their life, would describe a process that played out for them around food that aligned pretty closely with my version of events. To sum it up, I'll say that it's like we go into a kind of a self-induced hypnotic trance where we're able to justify behaviour that goes completely against the goal we're trying to achieve, because somehow, we manage to convince ourselves that we'll be able to do something tomorrow that for some reason we simply can't do today. Way back when I more or less yo-yo dieted my way through decades of my life, starting a new diet would be preceded by a great bacchanalian feast the day before, which I would justify by believing that by some superhuman act of will I would never eat anything unhealthy again from tomorrow and forever more.

Whilst a single episode like this would be bad enough, this kind of behaviour is particularly detrimental to anyone with a predisposition to getting stuck in vicious cycles of bingeing and restricting like I was for a big chunk of my life. In fact, this was the story of my life really from the age of about 12 until the age of 52. What happened at 52 was that I used myself as guinea pig in working out the wellness program that sat at the core of *Thrive in Midlife*. My sense was that I'd broken the back of that pattern of bingeing and starving through some pretty tough self-love and professional help that I called in at the time. But the fact is that I hadn't been on a diet or anything remotely like it since, and I was cautious about the possibility of triggering a relapse by starting to reign in the free form approach to eating that I'd taken to fully break my toxic patterns around food for once and for all.

I've got to say that I'm incredibly relieved to report that my concerns about relapsing when I started the trial of the Sirtfood approach that I'd been invited to be involved in turned out to be unfounded. In fact, it was a moment of truth for me when I realised that my disappointment about having put on close to 9kg in the two years since finishing *Thrive in Midlife* didn't cause me to rebound into a period of insane deprivation that my disordered thinking used to lead me to whenever I'd realise that the all-important number on the scales had gone up. In fact, I even felt kind of ok about it this time, because I could see that my weight had crept up without my really noticing it because I'd stopped compulsively weighing myself every day as I had done for many years previously. Thank god, I've finally got that monkey off my back. I've replaced it with a bevy of mindset and other tools that I now use to keep moving forward in terms of maintaining a healthy relationship with food, and in the process maintaining a healthy weight.

You might not completely fall in love with the Sirtfood approach like I did, but I feel confident that there is going to be something in this book that makes it easier for you to get to where you want to be in terms of your weight. My future is now looking really good, and yours can too if you approach the information I provide here with an open mind and a willingness to change. This will set you up to succeed much more surely than a closed mind and resistance to change ever could.

I can appreciate that you might be wondering why my weight piled on over the last couple of years given that I'd managed to get a handle on my problems with food. In retrospect, I can see that it was a case of having to take a step back to lay the foundations that would make it possible for me to keep moving forward. This is because it took time for me to tap back in to my appetite after decades of overriding it, and to retrain myself in terms of the reward signals that my brain had in place after years of using food for all of the wrong reasons. At the most basic level I can see in hindsight that my portion sizes and some of my food choices weren't ideal from the point of view of maintaining a healthy weight, but hey - I was on a steep learning curve in terms of becoming reacquainted with my body's signals around when to eat and when to stop, as well as how to deal with stress and uncomfortable emotions without resorting to bingeing.

Weighing myself for the Sirtfood trial brought the moment of truth about my weight gain out into the open where I could see it dispassionately for what it was. Fortunately, the opportunity to trial the Sirtfood approach under controlled conditions was a real gift because it gave me a clear sense of where I was at, both in terms of my weight and in terms of my mindset, and it gave me a safe and effective way to work toward achieving a healthier sustainable weight for myself moving forward.

So it's now been close to two years since I've 'acted out' in any obsessive or destructive ways around food. This is particularly gratifying given the fact that the years between writing *Thrive in Midlife* and this book haven't been easy ones for me. They included the challenge of having to handle the fall-out from being made redundant at the age of 52, and finding myself going into menopause at exactly the same time as my daughter was going into adolescence. Needless to say, the hormonal volcano that our house sat on top of over the last couple of years was a perfect testing ground for the mindset and stress management strategies that I developed for *Thrive in Midlife*. For me, stress used to inevitably lead to bingeing on high-sugar low-nutrition food to numb the range of feelings that would come up because of the emotional, psychological and physical changes my body underwent when it was stressed.

Ultimately, it's because I'd trained myself to manage my response to stress so well during 2014, that I didn't resort to using bingeing as a coping mechanism under the trying circumstances I found myself in.

More recently I've had the benefit of experiencing what eating a diet stacked with Sirtfoods can achieve. This has been an absolute game changer for me. I've never felt better, and I now feel well enough connected to my body's signals to be able to stay on the straight and narrow in terms of the amount and kinds of foods that I eat as I move through the last trimester of my life.

I love the emphasis that Goggin and Hatten put on things when they say that it's not about what you take off your plate, but what you put on it that counts. As I mentioned earlier, one of the great side effects of adopting this way of eating for me is that I've regained awareness of my body's signals around satiety and hunger. What's more, I've also regained the ability to really taste simple foods again. It's interesting how desensitised our taste buds become after periods of eating what we colloquially call 'comfort foods'. Don't get me wrong, there's nothing wrong with comfort, and there's nothing wrong with food. But if putting them together leads to sugar and chemical-filled processed products which it inevitably does, then you're going to find yourself needing more and more of the stuff to get the same hit of dopamine that you're unconsciously chasing. The scary thing is that this is what addiction looks like. You'll be reading more about how the body's reward system works later in this book. It is important to be aware of this phenomenon because if your reward system has been screwed up over time like mine was, you're going to be setting yourself up for failure in terms of maintaining a healthy weight if you launch into a diet of any kind without addressing what's going on in your body in relation to triggering the release of the feel-good chemicals like dopamine that are an integral part of your body's reward system. And make no mistake about it, it's your body's reward system that ultimately drives your behaviour. It's worth doing whatever it takes to realign it to help you toward your goal of reaching and maintaining your ideal weight.

We're going to take a look at how our body works in the next chapter, so that you have that information to anchor everything in the following chapters, to the fundamental biochemistry that determines whether your body will be well or not.

CHAPTER TWO

The Body Factor

This chapter is all about giving you a basic level of understanding about:

- the body's processes for getting energy from food,
- the body's processes for eliminating waste,
- the role of hormones, and
- what happens to our brain when we combine a stress-filled life, with the wrong kinds of food, and chronic dieting.

I've included this material so that you can appreciate why treating your body well in relation to what you eat, and why the amount of weight you carry is so important. An overarching principle in all of this is that the body's processes are aimed at achieving homeostasis. Homeostasis is the word used to describe internal stability. The rationale for the recommendations in the following chapters are based on the fact that not turning around any poor lifestyle habits you're harbouring will greatly increase your chance of struggling through midlife and beyond. That's because your body will be forced to work way too hard to maintain the degree of homeostasis it needs to have in place to function well.

We start by taking a look at what goes on in our cells because they are the fundamental building blocks of the body. Specifically, it's the way cells access energy that sheds light on how much control we have around the way we feel, look and age.

Oxygen is critical to the process of generating energy as it helps metabolise the nutrients released from food during digestion. But this process of releasing energy is a double-edged sword, because oxidation results from oxygen coming into contact with anything, and oxidation damages our cell membranes and the other structures that are vital to our health and wellbeing.

Meanwhile, oxidants are critical to our health because of the free radicals they produce. These free radicals help to kill invading bacteria as part of the immune system. Free radicals have developed a bad reputation as a result of the way vitamin supplements and the like are advertised. But it turns out that they're actually critical to our immune system's ability to fight off disease. It's when we have more free radicals than our body can handle that we get into trouble.

A free radical is any kind of atom with at least one unpaired electron in its outer cell. Atoms need a pair of electrons to be stable. If there aren't two present, the atom will seek out another electron to achieve stability. It effectively steals this from another molecule, which causes the other molecule to become unstable. The problem with free radicals is that damage occurs to the body when unstable molecules float around looking for another electron to pair with instead of staying where they're meant to be. So if the molecule was part of a cell wall for example, the wall will be damaged as the molecule separates from it in search of another electron. A big problem here is that the most likely part of the cell to be attacked when the cell wall is damaged is the DNA. This matters because the genetic information in the DNA is the code that runs every process in our body.

As well as being produced naturally by the body's own processes, free radicals also result from the environment we live in, with things like poor air quality, fast food, chemicals, preservatives, smoking, and stress significantly contributing to the free radical load present in our body at any one time. So, if our lifestyle results in the balance of oxidants and antioxidants being disturbed to the extent that our DNA is damaged, over time we'll start to experience health issues of one kind or other.

Antioxidants which are either produced by our body or taken in when we eat, are thought to prevent some of the damage done by free radicals by neutralising them with a spare electron that pairs with their lone one. Antioxidants are the only molecules that don't become unstable when they lose an electron. This is why they are so important to maintaining good health. It's not surprising then that the Sirtfood approach is full of foods that are high in antioxidants.

You'll find out more about how to dramatically increase your intake of antioxidants using Sirtfoods in the next chapter, but before we get to that point we're going to take a closer look at the way the digestive system works, because it will help you to understand why diet is so important from the point of view of how you feel, how you age, and how you experience the disruption to the balance of hormones that both men and women experience during the midlife phase.

In fact, research over the past two decades has revealed that a well-functioning digestive system, colloquially known as the gut, is absolutely critical to good health. There have been whole books written on the topic because it's now understood that problems as varied as diabetes, obesity, rheumatoid arthritis, autism spectrum disorder, depression and chronic fatigue syndrome can all be improved dramatically by addressing issues around gut health.

You can think of the gut as being like a complicated tube that passes from the mouth to the anus, with anything you eat that isn't fully digested passing right through from one end to the other. One of the most important functions of the gut is to prevent toxic substances generated through the digestion of food from entering the blood stream and circulating around the body. As a critical part of the immune system, the gut is also instrumental in defending the body against non-food related pathogens as well. Our gut is home to some 100 trillion microorganisms that make up the environment that keeps us well as long as it hasn't become degraded as a result of using antibiotics or via any number of other ways in which our gut flora can become unbalanced. Leaky Gut Syndrome for example is a very serious problem because it results in toxic substances being released into the blood stream and circulating around our body.

The things we do to influence the incredible internal ecosystem that comprises our gut starts when we put food into our mouth and start to chew it. Do you remember being told to chew your food well as a kid?

That's because that's where food starts to be prepared to both contribute to and benefit from the complex intestinal environment I mentioned above.

After we swallow, the food makes its way into our stomach where it's mixed with the specific acids and enzymes that break it down so that it can be digested. This involves the carbohydrate in the food for example, being broken down into glucose to be released into the bloodstream where it's available to be used for energy either immediately, or stored away for use at a later time. Insulin is critical to this process. That's why a lack of insulin or insulin resistance is such a big issue. A particularly worrying trend that's been building since processed foods came onto the scene in the 1950's, is that increasing numbers of people are being diagnosed with type 2 diabetes. Approximately 280 Australians develop type 2 diabetes every day, with almost 1.7 million Australians currently living with the condition.

Diabetes comes about either as a result of our body halting or slowing down the production of insulin, or developing resistance to it. When everything is working well though, insulin is released from the pancreas when it's required, and transported through the bloodstream signalling to the cells to let the glucose in. Blood sugar levels then start to drop as glucose moves from the bloodstream into the cells, and this signals the pancreas to reduce the amount of insulin it's releasing, which in turn results in the amount of glucose going into the cells decreasing. This balancing act happens many times throughout the day as energy is called on or stored. In fact, it's a perfect example of the way the body maintains homeostasis.

One thing to keep in mind when you're reading the next chapter and thinking about the kinds of foods to include in your diet to help you to manage your weight and age well, is that our ability to control our blood sugar levels decreases as we age. It's also important to be aware of the fact that we start producing more advanced glycation end products or AGEs as we get older as well. AGEs are harmful by-products of the process the body uses to make energy from glucose. The problem with AGEs is that they attach to and damage the proteins in our skin and our arteries, causing them to become stiffer and less effective. So AGEs not only contribute to our looking older via the wrinkling of our skin, but they also predispose us to more serious problems like cardiovascular disease by hardening our arteries. As mentioned above, AGEs are made in small quantities as a by-product of the body's processes for metabolising sugar, with the problems really starting to hit home when the body becomes overloaded with them if we eat a lot of processed foods. This is because the processing methods that make these foods digestible, tasty, and able to be stored for long periods of time, raises the AGEs in them to levels that are dangerous for our body.

The body responds to AGEs like it responds to an infection, with a low level of inflammation arising when they are present in our body. There's both a cause and an effect scenario at play here. On the one hand, we can see that inflammation is one of the key factors that actually ages us, while at the same time simply getting older results in more inflammation in our body as well.

Millennia ago, a strong immune and inflammatory response was key to humans surviving to the age where reproduction is possible. So, from an evolutionary perspective it makes perfect sense that this is how the body operates in terms of its immune system. Meanwhile. it's a problem for us now because we live for extended periods, and it's the very same response mechanisms that were responsible for the survival of the human race way back when, that slowly lead to our organs losing their functionality and/or their structural integrity as we age. In turn it's this loss of functionality and structural integrity that ultimately leads to age-related diseases like dementia, cancer, heart disease, stroke, arthritis, kidney disease, and type 2 diabetes. This is ironic for sure, but I don't want to detract from the fact that if you maintain a diet that results in AGEs building up to the extent that they cause excessive inflammation in your body, you'll slowly but surely be setting yourself up to age much faster than you otherwise would.

There are plenty of reasons for putting time and effort in to managing your weight, not least of which is the fact that fat cells themselves are capable of creating chemical signals that lead to chronic inflammation. What happens here is that if you habitually consume more calories than your body needs, some of your fat cells will expand to increase their capacity to store the excess calories you're taking in as fat. They literally 'turn on' when this happens, and in the process, add to the inflammation that's already present. The point is that you can switch this process off again by eating sensibly, and losing weight which allows the fat cells to turn off the signals that trigger the chronic inflammation.

Then there's the matter of how our body eliminates waste when the food we've eaten makes its way down to the other end of the digestive system to consider. Defecation is the word given to the process that removes indigestible and therefore toxic materials from our body so that they don't build up in our gut and cause us to get sick. Meanwhile our body is 60% water, and just as defecation takes wastes products out of our body, so too the body has the process of urination which serves to flush the toxins it carries out of the body in fluid form to keep us well.

To maintain homeostasis of course we need to replace the fluid in our body all of the time. In fact, failing to consume adequate amounts of water is just as problematic as failing to consume adequate amounts of fibre. So, it's worrying to note that many people don't drink the recommended 2 litres of water every day, or include enough foods that are high in both soluble and insoluble fibre in their diet. It's important to consume around 25g of fibre every day to keep our digestive system working well. One of the main causes of constipation is not eating enough fruit and vegetables that provide our system with enough soluble fibre to soften our stools and make them easier to pass. Meanwhile insoluble fibre passes through our digestive system without being broken down and helps other foods move through the process of being digested more easily.

So, what is the role of hormones in all of this then? It turns out that they actually play a huge role because hormones are the chemical substances made by our organs to control all of the different functions in our body. Hormones are all about balance. For example, as we saw earlier, insulin is the hormone that is responsible for regulating the amount of glucose in our blood.

A couple of other important hormones that are involved in the digestive process are ghrelin and leptin. Leptin is the hormone that signals satiety and ghrelin is the hormone that stimulates appetite. Ghrelin also stimulates the release of growth hormone, and plays a role in the control of insulin release. Leptin on the other hand tells the brain to do a variety of things including stimulating the breakdown of white fat. It is most well known for being the hormone that signals when we've had enough to eat. In other words, leptin is the hormone behind that feeling of being full.

Menopause is one of the life phases in which we're likely to become acutely aware of the impact of fluctuations in our hormone levels. Perimenopause is the stage before menopause that can begin as early as the 30s in some women. This is the stage where the ovaries start to make less oestrogen, and it tends to be in the latter stages of perimenopause that we start noticing the kinds of symptoms that we associate with menopause such as irregular periods, hot flushes, mood swings, anxiety, sleep problems, loss of libido, vaginal dryness, fatigue, lack of mental clarity, incontinence, aching joints and muscles, thinning hair, brittle fingernails and weight gain. As mentioned earlier, this is not a one-size-fits-all scenario, with some people barely being affected at all, while others experience the onset of menopause as downright earth shattering.

There is debate around whether male menopause is actually a 'thing', but the fact is that testosterone levels do in fact decline with age in both men and women, and some men experience symptoms including sexual dysfunction, fatigue, weakness, depression and weight gain as a result of the declining levels of testosterone.

This chapter is all about giving you a snapshot of the kinds of things you need to keep in mind when considering the role that your behaviour around food in particular has in helping your body to stay well. I included this material because I figure that without taking our power back and informing ourselves about what's going on inside our bodies, we risk the possibility of serious decline in our quality of life as we age. The vested interests of the multinationals running the food and pharmaceutical industries suggest that whilst going with the path of least resistance might be easy, it is definitely not in our own best interests.
If I've learnt anything over the years, I've learnt that overpowering your desire for food is not what maintaining a healthy weight is all about. In other words, success is not dependent on willpower alone. And in fact, we now know about the impact of things like stress and lack of sleep on our ability to even access willpower, not to mention the impact of

what Dilia Suriel who wrote *The Thin Woman's Brain* explains as "our struggle to lose weight is caused by the dieting cycle and other factors that have modified our brains to become food-obsessed". What we now know about neuroplasticity explains why it is that some of us wind up spending our lives swinging between starvation and bingeing before we work out how to use the neuroplasticity that keeps us stuck in the trap, to get ourselves back out of it again.

The following chapters will augment this basic information that I've provided you with about the body's processes for getting energy from food and eliminating waste, and the role that hormones play in keeping our bodies ticking over well. As you read on, you'll be learning about the effects of stress, diet, exercise, and mindset, on all of the above.

CHAPTER THREE

The Food Factor

I'll be filling you in on the foods that are included in the SirtFood protocol that I got such wonderful results from at the end of 2016 toward the end of this chapter. But for now, we are going to step back and focus on the main food groups so that we've got a common foundational understanding of what our options are here. These main food groups are carbohydrates, fats, and proteins.

CARBOHYDRATES:

Carbohydrates are the essential fuel of the central nervous system. They're actually the most efficient energy source our body can access, equating to 4 calories per gram. Carbohydrates should account for about half of our daily dietary intake with as much of this as possible being in the complex form. Unfortunately, many of us have a history of loading our bodies with way too many refined simple carbohydrates that lead to spikes in our blood sugar. These spikes result in the release of insulin that is responsible for moving the sugar from our blood and into our cells where it can be used for energy.

When I wrote *Thrive in Midlife* I expressed gratitude to Christiane Northrup who wrote *The Wisdom of Menopause*. I want to mention her again here because she's a down-to-earth straight talker when it comes to explaining some of the physical processes that go on in our bodies when we eat the wrong kinds of food, combined with other lifestyle factors that don't serve us well. For example, she explains that our metabolism slows right down as our bodies become more efficient at storing fat because of the level of stress in our lives in general, and in particular the stress that our bodies are under when our blood sugar levels are way too high.

The long and the short of it is that our blood sugar levels get too high when we eat too many simple carbohydrates. Simple carbohydrates are the ones found in processed foods like cakes, biscuits, most breads and breakfast cereals. Complex carbohydrates on the other hand, are the ones found in foods like oatmeal, rice, and some vegetables. They take much longer to digest than simple carbohydrates, and result in our blood sugar levels rising much more gradually. The carbohydrates in the Sirtfood approach are not only efficient in this regard, but also because they come from foods that stimulate our sirtuin gland, and thus set off a chain reaction of processes that can undo some of the damage we may have been doing to our body through the consumption of processed and junk foods that are laden with simple carbohydrates.

The other problem to be aware of in relation to simple carbohydrates is that the changes they undergo during processing results in high levels of the damaging AGEs that we talked about in the last chapter. As a recovered junk food addict myself, I have to say that AGEs have played a disproportionally important role in my life up until a couple of years ago. That's a real problem for a number of reasons. Not only did I waste a lot of time and energy obsessing over food, and either restricting or bingeing on it, but also on a physical level it set me up for a future plagued with health issues. The bottom line is that excessive inflammation and elevated blood sugar levels from consuming the wrong foods cause inflammation in the lining of the blood vessels, and can go on to become what's known as Syndrome X. Syndrome X is a precursor to type 2 diabetes. Personally, I'm incredibly grateful that I found out what I needed to know to put a stop to things before they got to that point, because there's no doubt in my mind whatsoever that that was where I was heading.

I used the reasons behind the strategies I put into the 42-day program that I built *Thrive in Midlife* around to get myself motivated. Gaining an understanding of the role of glucose in transporting energy into the cells where it's used for fuel was a really effective deterrent for me from the point of view of my less than healthy habits around food at the time, because it helped me to see why my body would work so much better on a diet of unrefined whole foods that include carbohydrates from fruits, vegetables, and whole grains, rather than the unnaturally sweetened and flavoured processed foods that I used to crave and binge on.

This book will help you to be much more aware of what's at stake if you're someone like me who trained your body to crave the wrong kinds of food from a very young age. It will also give you strategies to support you through what can initially be a very difficult process if you decide like me, that you're prepared to do whatever it takes to set yourself up for a future free from unnecessary illness by getting sugar and processed foods out of your life. Changing from a predominantly processed food to a predominantly whole food diet is incredibly challenging for many people for a number of reasons, not least of which is because refined sugar is one of the most addictive substances in the world.

Needless to say, breaking my addiction to sugar back in 2014 was a real game changer for me. But I have to admit that I still hanker for sweet tastes. I usually satisfy this with a bit of stevia. Stevia is a natural plant based sweetener that has none of the toxic substances that artificial sweeteners have. That said, it is still in my best interest to train myself to appreciate the natural flavours in food, because even though stevia doesn't have any of the toxic side effects of chemicals like aspartame that is used in artificial sweeteners, clinical trials have shown that there is still a downside in that both chemical and non-chemical sweeteners boost hunger by activating the appetite pathways in our body. The way I look at it is that I'm still a bit of a work in progress in relation to my health transformation.

The opposite of sweet is astringent, and I have to say that my introduction to the very astringent vegetables that are the heroes of the Sirtfood approach came as a bit of a shock to my system. If you're not sure of what astringency is, think of a juice made of parsley, kale, celery, lemon, ginger, and green apples, and you've got the liquid definition of astringency. This combination is one of the foundations of the Sirtfood protocol. There's no two ways about it, I hated the Sirtfood juice when I first tried it, and without hesitation I continue to resort to adding some stevia to make it more palatable. The bottom line for me is that I love the fact that drinking a juice like this every morning is a super quick and easy way to activate my sirtuin gene, and if a little bit of stevia is going to get me over the line, it's a price I'm prepared to pay at the moment.

Some of you might be wondering where the glycaemic index (GI) fits in with all of this. The glycaemic index (GI) is another way of working out what you should and shouldn't eat in terms of your diet's impact on your blood sugar levels. To get a handle on how the glycaemic index can help, simply think of favouring foods that are known as low GI foods and limiting the high GI foods as much as possible. Like simple carbohydrates, high GI foods break down quickly and result in spikes in blood sugar. Low GI foods on the other hand are broken down much more slowly and raise blood sugar levels much less dramatically, thus requiring less insulin to metabolize them. Low GI foods include things like oats, brown rice, some breads and some fruits and vegetables. If you're using the GI approach to work out what to include in your diet, remember to choose foods that are as close to their natural state as possible. On a cautionary note, I want to warn you that some of the foods that are ranked as low GI are still laced with preservatives and artificial flavours and sweeteners that are no good for our body at all. And again, the processing of these products results in the production of AGEs as well.

Another unfortunate side effect of highly processing grains is that the fibre they contain naturally is lost in the process. Fibre is incredibly important from the point of view of our overall health. Having adequate amounts of fibre in our diet to keep our bowels working well, and also helps to reduce the level of bad cholesterol in our blood, whilst at the same time slowing down the rate of digestion so that much less insulin is released in the process. It also results in our feeling fuller for longer as well, so it's also helpful from the point of view of managing our weight.

The sad fact is that too many people suffer from problems in relation to the elimination of waste from their bodies because the processed foods that they fill their diet with lack adequate amounts of fibre. Studies have shown that most Australians do not consume the recommended daily intake of 25 grams of fibre. If you're one of these people you need to know that sooner or later this way of eating is going to start causing problems by hampering your body's natural detoxification processes. If your digestive system is sluggish in this regard, the simple prescription is to include more fibre in your diet, drink more water, and do more exercise. If this doesn't work for you, it's worth seeking the help of a health professional sooner rather than later to see if you've got an underlying problem that needs to be addressed. It stands to reason that you're not going to be able to function at your best if the toxins created in the digestive process remain in your body for longer than they should.

These days there's little doubt about the mind/body connection, but I guess I've tended to be more interested in the way the mind affects the body rather than the other way around at least until relatively recently. I now see that there are equally important things to be found out about the way the body affects the mind. In fact, it's now known that the gut actually sends more messages to the brain than the brain sends to the gut. What really surprised me when I started looking into this is that 90% of the body's serotonin receptors are located in the gut. The fact that serotonin is the neurotransmitter that's central to our ability to feel happy and well, brings into question the levels of antidepressants being prescribed these days. Would it surprise you to know that Australia was ranked second behind Finland in a recent snapshot of antidepressant usage across the 36 OECD nations? This comes about because 89 out of every 1,000 people in Australia is being prescribed with antidepressants. I wonder how different this statistic might be if more doctors looked at what's going on in someone's gut when they present with depression, before they get their prescription pad out to offer a pharmacological solution. I'm not suggesting that there's no place for anti-depressants, but I'm wondering whether there might be equally, if not more effective side effect free options that aren't being fully explored in the transaction between most doctors and their patients.

CHOLESTEROL:

The fact of the matter is that a predominantly whole food, high fibre diet not only leads to healthy levels of blood sugar and a healthier gut, but it also keeps our blood cholesterol low. We need some cholesterol to help maintain the health of our brain, skin, and other organs. But the fact is that too many of us have unhealthy levels of Low Density Lipoprotein or LDL. This predisposes us to coronary artery disease and stroke. Because of our estrogen levels prior to menopause, women generally have lower overall levels of cholesterol than men, however this evens out once we go into menopause when our decreasing level of estrogen results in a boost to our risk of developing problems with cholesterol. Estimates are that over 5.5 million Australians or one third of all adults over the age of 18 are courting disaster by living with dangerously high levels of cholesterol.

Cholesterol comes from the body itself and from the food that we eat. Some people are genetically disadvantaged as their bodies produce too much cholesterol in the first place. In others, it's the food they eat that causes the problems. In either case diet is important. Statins are the drug of choice if changes in lifestyle don't prove to be effective in bringing cholesterol levels to within a healthy range. But even if these drugs didn't come with some pretty negative potential side effects like muscle aches, difficulty sleeping, memory loss, and high blood sugar, I would still recommend sorting lifestyle issues out before resorting to taking drugs.

It's the LDL that we need to be lowering, because LDL is the one that carries cholesterol away from the liver and into the bloodstream. LDL is the one that's involved in the build-up of plaque that can clog the arteries leading to a greatly increased risk of heart attack or stroke. Whereas High Density Lipoprotein (HDL) is known as the good cholesterol because it removes LDL from where it can do damage and transports it to the liver where it is broken down to be excreted.

FATS:

Fats are the most energy dense of the food groups with 9 calories per gram. Fat is important for the body because it provides thermal insulation, and protects the vital organs from trauma. It carries the fat-soluble vitamins to where they need to be, as well as being involved in the production of many regulatory hormones. Fat is also involved in brain development and function. A healthy diet from the point of view of cholesterol includes limiting saturated and trans fats, and including healthy fats like coconut and olive oil. Olive oil is one of the core Sirtfoods. It's also one of the main reason that the Mediterranean Diet is so health enhancing as well. Saturated and trans fats are the ones you want to steer clear of. They are found in baked goods like cookies and cakes, and fried foods like chips. Ultimately you should aim for your diet to be made up of absolutely no more than 30% fat, with less than 10% of that coming from saturated fats.

The problem with transfats is that they lower the good HDL cholesterol in the blood and increase the bad LDL cholesterol. On the other hand, polyunsaturated fats like omega 3 and omega 6 oils are much healthier. Among other things, they help to reduce our risk of heart disease and increase the health of our brain. A healthy balanced diet should include the healthier polyunsaturated fats and monounsaturated fats that are found in foods like avocados, oily fish, almonds, and cooking oils made from plants or seeds. As far as the Sirtfood approach is concerned, extra virgin olive oil and walnuts are the non-plant based heroes that are incredibly effective at activating our sirtuin genes.

Omega 6 is found in foods like oily fish, tahini, linseed, flax seed, pine nuts, and brazil nuts. Omega 6 fats also contribute Vitamin E, which is a powerful antioxidant and can have a beneficial effect on our heart. On a cautionary note though, it's important not to consume them to excess. Both omega 6 and omega 3 fats are precursors to other substances involved in regulating blood pressure, and the body's inflammatory response. This means that they can offset some of the damaging processes we are exposed to as we age. In particular Omega 6 in moderation has also been seen to ease some of the symptoms of menopause. Omega 3 fish oils are the heroes of the Sirtfood approach as far as fats are concerned because as Goggin and Hatton say "as well as having numerous benefits to health in their own right, these oils also appear to favourably influence the way our sirtuin genes work."

PROTEIN:

Protein is the other main food group we need to consider to get a picture of what a healthy diet looks like. Protein is part of every tissue in our body, and because our body can't produce it itself, we need to consume adequate amounts in our diet. Protein is not only important because it is central to our ability to build and repair tissue, but also because it is made up of leucine which enhances the way Sirtfoods work.

Like carbohydrates, protein has 4 calories per gram. In addition to building and repairing tissue, protein is also important from the point of view of our immune system. To maintain a healthy body, adult women need to consume 46 grams of protein and adult men need to consume 56 grams of protein every day. Animal products such as meats, milk, fish, and eggs are rich sources of protein, but as they are also major sources of cholesterol it's important to make sure that you balance your diet by consuming protein that is found in plant and other non-animal sources as well. These sources include soybeans, legumes, nut butters, and some grains such as wheat germ and quinoa. According to the Sirtfood approach, buckwheat is a brilliant alternative to grains especially for anyone who's gluten intolerant. People think buckwheat is a grain but it's actually a fruit seed. It has 13g of protein per 100. This is equal to the amount of protein in eggs. As far as animal sources of protein go, it's important to trim the fat off meat, and favour chicken and fish over red meat. It's also important to avoid the production of AGEs by slow cooking, stewing or steaming your meat rather than grilling and barbequing it at high temperatures.

Knowing everything that I now know about what our bodies need to be well, I'm confident in recommending that you follow a wholefood approach to eating, with everything that passes your lips being in as close to its natural state as possible. The body thrives on a diet that is mostly plant based, with the fruit and vegetable foundation augmented by unprocessed complex carbohydrates, healthy fats, protein, fibre, vitamins, minerals, and water for hydration. You'll be minimizing damage from free radicals by including a wide range of foods that supply an adequate amount and range of antioxidants. One of the great benefits of the Sirtfood approach that I go into in more detail soon, is that it includes foods that are not only high in antioxidants, but are also effective at activating the body's sirtuin genes that speed up our metabolism and initiate a number of changes to the way our cells operate that are beneficial from an anti-ageing point of view.

When I look back over my history with food, my first impulse is to look away. It's not a pretty picture I'm afraid. As far as weight loss is concerned, it feels like I've tried every diet under the sun. One of the many traps I fell into in the quest to be skinny when I was younger, was to dive headfirst into the high-protein diets that were all the rage a while back. Certainly, understanding the importance of protein was a really significant and positive learning for me, but the way I embraced the extremely high protein regimes like the Atkins and HCG diets was anything but healthful. Prior to latching on to the high protein regimes, I was a great fan of the low-fat diets. These days it's well known how important consuming the right amount of the right fats is, but back in the day it was all about getting as much fat out of our diet as possible. Sure enough, these approaches were all effective in terms of losing weight in the short term, but what I didn't realize at the time was that the weight I was losing when I was on the low fat diets was achieved for the most part through the loss of muscle rather than the loss of fat. Meanwhile the problem with the high protein diets was that I was forcing my body to use protein for energy in the absence of adequate levels of carbohydrate and fat. The consequence of this was that I didn't get nearly as much muscle building and tissue repair from the protein I was consuming as I should have, because as Professor Roberta Anding describes it, "forcing the body to use protein as an energy source is like burning hundred dollar bills to heat your house". This is because the body will send the protein in the system to the liver so that the nitrate can be stripped from it to enable it to become a kind of de facto carbohydrate when there is not enough carbohydrate from the food we eat to transport energy to the cells. This means that the protein is no longer available for our body to use in building muscle and repairing tissue which is what it's really needed for.

One of the things I really struggled with during my years of using food for all of the wrong reasons was portion control. The sad thing about this is that there is a really effective volume sensor in the body that feeds us information about when to start and when to stop eating. The problem is that this doesn't work if we override it again and again, like I did with my compulsive cycle of bingeing and then starving when I was younger. It also isn't of much help if we fill up on calorie dense, but volume poor food which is what we inevitably do when processed foods are involved. Couple this with the fact that this volume sensor becomes less effective as we age, as does our ability to sense and regulate our blood sugar levels, and I think you can see how important it is to take an approach to life where our awareness around our body's needs in respect of nutrition remains high at all times. This is why I've given you a number of mindfulness-related exercises in the mindset chapter that's coming up. These are designed to help you to be able to stay present and accountable for what you put into your mouth. If you get your diet right, pretty soon you'll start feeling better. You'll look healthier and younger, and you'll start sleeping more soundly. You'll have more zest for life, and you'll be slowing down the ageing process as well. Also, I know for a fact that when I'm eating a wholefood plant-based diet with minimal processed foods in it, I don't suffer the classic menopause symptoms of hot flushes, aching joints, and mood swings nearly as much as I do when I'm eating poorly.

Eating in a way that doesn't support your body to function well will leave you feeling lacklustre and drained. It will speed up the aging process, and predispose you to developing preventable diseases like diabetes, heart disease, blood pressure, arthritis, and the list goes on. And in at least some cases as in my own, it will also exacerbate menopausal symptoms like hot flushes as well.

When I wrote *Thrive in Midlife* it was clear that I could make a big difference to my wellbeing if I made sure that I got bang for my buck in terms of what I put into my mouth. In addition to the general understanding I had back then, I now know that it's worth being even more focussed to ensure that I increase the level of sirtuin activating antioxidants in my diet to the best of my ability as well. I initially included these to help me to move some of the excess weight I'd put on since finishing *Thrive in Midlife*. Now that the excess weight is gone, I just can't think of a good reason to stop loading my body up with these power packed foods that do such great things from the point of view of my overall health.

SIRTFOODS:

So, let's take a closer look at what's involved in the Sirtfood protocol that proved to be so incredibly effective in helping me to move the excess weight I'd put on between finishing "Thrive in Midlife" in 2014 and starting to write this book toward the end of 2016. As far as concrete results are concerned I can report that the initial, fairly hard core phase of the protocol was pretty amazing. Within a week of starting I'd lost over 3 kilos, and within a month I'd lost a bit under 7. I really wasn't expecting this given that I'm at a time in life when it's notoriously difficult for women in particular to lose weight. The long and the short of it is, that this great result came about because of the way Sirtfoods activate our sirtuin gene. This is the gene that's recently been shown to function in a way that promotes anti-aging and weight loss by forcing our body to use fat for energy and eliminate cellular debris from our cells.

I'd never even heard of the sirtuin gene prior to being introduced to Goggin and Haddon's book. But I was familiar with the effectiveness of fasting diets like the 5:2. What I didn't know at the time was that diets like this also work because they activate our sirtuin gene. They do this because an increased amount of stress is placed on our body when energy in the form of food is in short supply. This stress is then sensed by the sirtuins that respond by sending out powerful signals that radically alter the way our cells behave. This is where the magic happens. Our metabolism is ramped up. Our muscles become more efficient. Our body's natural fat burning mechanism is switched on, inflammation is reduced, and the repair of damaged cells starts happening. This is fantastic stuff. In fact, it's not so dissimilar to the way our body operates when it's young.

Goggins and Matten developed the Sirtfood regime because they knew that consuming a diet that is rich in Sirtfoods is a much more sustainable and effective way of activating the sirtuin gene than fasting. Sirtfoods have the power to do what they do because they are high in natural plant chemicals called polyphenols. You'll know which plants are high in polyphenols because they are likely to have a high degree of astringency. For example, green apples activate the sirtuin gene whilst red apples do not. While we're on the question of astringency, I'll never forget the first sip I had of the green juice that forms the central platform of the Sirtfood regime. It's made up of things like kale, celery, rocket, lemon, parsley and matcha, which is essentially green tea leaves that are ground into a fine powder. Frankly it was barely palatable for me at first, so as I said earlier, I resolved to cope with the astringent taste of this brew by adding a couple of drops of stevia to take the edge off it. Otherwise I think I might have had to abandon the project altogether which would have been a real shame given the results I got in terms of weight loss in the short term, and the results I continue to get in terms of weight management and wellbeing overall.

Fortunately, not only didn't I abandon the project, but I pretty much followed the diet to the letter. That involved a fairly hard-core initial phase where I restricted my intake of calories to a maximum of 1000 per day for the first three days. This consisted of three Sirtfood-rich green juices per day, plus one full meal that was rich in Sirtfoods every day.

The period after the amazing but pretty challenging first three days involves restricting your intake to 1500 calories a day that you get from two Sirtfood-rich green juices and two Sirtfood-rich meals.

Week 2 is the beginning of phase 2 which is a 14-day period where no calorie counting as such is required, while you focus on consuming three balanced Sirtfood-rich meals each day, along with a Sirtfood green juice for maintenance. I'm so glad that I bought the SirtFood Recipe Book when I started the trial. I really enjoyed trying the recipes out, and can highly recommend the lentil soup and various tasty curries that you'll find recipes for in the book.

Lastly, I don't want you to think that starting off with the protocol full-on like I did is mandatory. You'll still get fantastic results if you simply start filling your shopping trolley with Sirtfoods as soon as possible.

So here is a list of some of the core Sirtfoods:

- Walnuts
- Strawberries
- Coffee
- Kale

- Celery
- Extra-virgin olive oil
- Buckwheat
- Birdseye chilli
- Cocoa

Then, there are second tier Sirtfoods which include things like:

- Artichokes
- Apples
- Chestnuts
- Quinoa
- Broad beans
- Chives
- Black and white tea

I've purposely truncated the information I'm providing you with here out of respect for Goggin and Haddon who carried out the research and have the credentials to substantiate the recommendations in the protocol. What I want to say is that if you plan to start amping up your use of Sirtfoods, I recommend you get the *SirtFood Diet Recipe Book* that contains among other things a complete list of the foods that rate well. I've never been a great cook myself, and these days I feel really blessed to have a brilliant range of super-healthy meals that I can make for my family with a minimum of fuss and maximum benefit it terms of taste and health enhancement. Notwithstanding the fact that my mindset is dramatically improved in relation to self-care, the difference between my experience of the Sirtfood approach and the plethora of other diets I've been on in the past, is the fact that I simply can't think of a single good reason to stop eating this way. There is no deprivation involved, no hunger, and a general feeling of wellbeing that I've really never had before. This is why I'm including this information in a book that is essentially recommending that you avoid dieting in preference for treating your body well in respect of what you eat on a day-by-day basis. To this end, I offer you the following general principles to set you on the right track:

- Eat mindfully.
- Avoid processed foods as much as possible.
- Consume around 46 grams of protein every day if you are a woman and 56 grams of protein every day if you're a man.
- Consume at least 25 grams of fibre every day.
- Aim for carbohydrates to account for about half of your dietary intake with as much as possible being in the complex form.
- Minimize your intake of simple carbohydrates.
- Include as much antioxidant rich food in your diet as possible, with at least 5 serves of vegetables and 2 serves of fruit per day, or better still, give the Sirtfood approach a go.
- Limit fats to less than 30% of total calories intake with trans fats accounting for less than 10% of your total fat consumption.
- Consistently exercise portion control.

- Cook using steaming or slow cooking rather than the high heat methods of grilling, frying, and barbequing.
- Drink at least two litres of water per day.
- Have a professional analyse the health of your gut, and take any recommended action to increase healthy gut flora seriously.

CHAPTER FOUR

The Mindset Factor

I'm indebted to Carol Dweck who wrote *Mindset: The New Psychology of Success*. She has provided a simple framework to help tease out the fundamentals of how it is that some people are predisposed to see their glass as half full while others see theirs as half empty. This chapter is all about working on your mindset so that it supports you to make any changes you need to make to set yourself on a path to lose excess weight, and to maintain a healthy weight moving forward. It's well worth the effort because it's critical to your ability to minimise your chances of succumbing to one or more of the largely preventable diseases that go hand in hand with eating the wrong kinds of food.

What you need to take on board from the get-go is the fact that your ability to accept responsibility for your outcomes is key here. The problem is that this is not an easy proposition for many people to accept. Among other things, it goes right to the heart of the characteristics of fixed versus growth mindsets that Carol Dweck's name is synonymous with. I've chosen to delve into this question of mindset by chunking it up to use Dweck's framework that approaches the question from the perspective of two overarching paradigms that our lives are played out in, because among other things, our ability to come to terms with the question of personal responsibility depends on where we sit on the fixed vs growth spectrum.

People who primarily operate from a fixed mindset believe that they are born with talents and tendencies in some areas and not others, and furthermore, that the tendencies they are born with are more or less the ones they go to the grave with. You'll hear people with fixed mindsets say things like, "I'm not one of those people who can eat one piece of chocolate and leave the rest of the block", or "I've always been lazy, I'll never get into the swing of exercising to stay fit". There's a sense for people operating from a fixed mindset that this is the way things are and that it's the way things will always be. It's underpinned by a belief that we don't have any personal agency and therefore can't be held accountable for the way things pan out. I guess that's actually true in one sense, because if you choose to believe that this is the way thing are, then sure enough that's the way they will be for you.

Thinking about the difference between fixed and growth mindsets reminds me of something my father said to me when I was a child. What he said was that "we can't do anything about the cards we're dealt, but it's up to us to decide which cards we play". This kind of worldview implies both opportunities to grow and improve, as well as responsibility for taking the action required to allow that growth to happen, whether that means signing up with a personal trainer or a nutritionist, or going back to university to retrain for a new career that requires specific qualifications. What I'm getting at here is that there's no need to let your history determine your future. Human beings are infinitely adaptable, and taking this point of view on board can mean the difference between leading a happy and healthy life, or not.

It's important to note how dynamic this matter of mindset actually is. It's possible that you approach some areas of your life from a fixed mindset, and others from a growth mindset, and it's also possible that you approach a certain area of your life from a fixed mindset sometimes, and then from a growth mindset at others.

What I want you to think about now is which mindset you're approaching the question of looking after your health and working your way toward a healthy weight from. Are you buzzing with excitement about seeing how good you will feel when you amp up the amount of Sirtfoods in your diet, or from making some other adjustment to the way you're eating? Or are you reading this book thinking that "it's all very well for some people who obviously have nerves of steel and tons of willpower, but I've never been able to take weight off and keep it off, and I probably never will"?

Obviously if you fall into the second category you're operating from a fixed mindset. If this is you, I want to urge you to take the time to reflect on exactly what it is that's stopping you from recognising that you can change, and recognising that changing the way you relate to food and exercise is critical to your ability to be well moving forward.

Unlike people operating from a fixed mindset, people operating from a growth mindset approach challenges with a high degree of curiosity and optimism. They tend to remain open to learning about new things throughout their life. They regard themselves as being empowered to improve no matter what their starting point is. Sure, they might never be able to make it to the Olympics or become a Rhodes scholar, but they know that they can improve in relation to anything that they put their mind to. It's about improvement for people with a growth mindset, not perfection.

As Dweck explains, it all comes down to the question of how we react to challenges. Do we just give up when we're challenged because we can't stand to risk failing, or do we keep working away in the knowledge that our failures are just stepping stones to success? A growth mindset allows for the idea that hard work and persistence always pays off in terms of our ability to continue to increase our skill in relation to any and all areas of our life.

The good news I have to share with you here is that no matter where you are on the fixed/growth continuum, you can strengthen your ability to operate from a growth mindset if you're prepared to do what it takes to turn your perspective around.

According to Dweck, strengthening your growth mindset starts with becoming aware of the language of your fixed mindset, and recognizing that you ultimately have a choice in relation to how you react to the circumstances of your life. Then whenever you hear yourself saying something like "I'm middle aged now and everybody knows that it's all but impossible to take the excess weight I'm carrying around off in middle age, so what's the point of even trying?", you need to engage the language of your growth mindset to refute what your fixed mindset is saying. After you've done that, you then need to go on to take the kind of action a person operating from a growth mindset would take. If you continue to be persistent in this regard, you'll slowly but surely reprogram your mind, alter your brain, and change your life forever.

So, the strategy that Dweck recommends if you ever need to move from a fixed mindset to a growth mindset is:

1. Notice fixed mindset thinking as it emerges.
2. Recognise that you a have choice in relation to how you think about the world and your place in it.
3. Counter your fixed mindset thinking with growth mindset thinking.
4. Take growth mindset action.
5. Repeat steps 1 to 4 as required.

The beauty of being human is that we're infinitely flexible. As Norman Doidge explains in his great book, *The Brain That Changes Itself*, we literally change our brain as we learn new things. In other words, the phenomenon known as neuroplasticity means that our behaviours are not hardwired into our brain, but rather they can be strengthened or weakened depending on the actions we take.

Very young children tend to naturally operate from a growth mindset. You can see them exploring their world with lots of curiosity and no fear of failure whatsoever. But most of us unlearn this perspective to some degree or other as we move through our lives in families, schools and workplaces that are more likely to reward us for what we achieve, rather than the attitude we work through challenges with. Research clearly shows that those who are consistently rewarded for doing their best, and persisting with tasks that they find challenging, not only go on to build strengths in relation to focus and perseverance, but also develop critical life skills like resilience. Whereas those who are only praised for their talent, their intelligence, and getting high grades, are not exposed to the same opportunities to develop these kinds of life enhancing skills. Worse still, they're at risk of associating their worth with their achievements, in which case failure of any kind is a terribly frightening prospect that leads to behaviours that are seriously limiting in terms of opportunities for growth. This is a vicious cycle that makes it easy to appreciate why people in the latter group are more likely to operate from a fixed mindset.

The simple fact is that if you take control of your mind rather than having it control you, you'll experience much more joy in your life. You'll experience much more peace of mind. You'll improve your health, your relationships, and your prospects of a happy and healthy future as you move through midlife and beyond. When you think about the fact that the huge diet industry is estimated to be worth over $20 billion a year in the US alone, it's not hard to see that there's something really powerful that gets between knowing what we should be eating to stay well, and what we actually dish up on our plates. In other words, understanding the decisions around what we do and do not eat, and whether we exercise regularly or not, is a pretty complex matter. Notwithstanding the fact that the advice we've been fed around diet over the last few decades has been crazy, confusing, contradictory, and often downright wrong, it's incumbent on us to tease out what's behind our less than ideal decisions about what we eat, so that we can move on and make the kinds of decisions that are going to enable us to achieve and maintain a healthy weight moving forward.

The fly in the ointment here is that there are people who seem to be able to 'naturally' maintain a healthy weight no matter what they do. One thing that these people have in common is that they are in touch with their body's signals and adept at responding to them. I don't have any statistics at hand, but my hunch is that there are many more people who either regularly override their body's signals, or aren't even aware of them in the first place. I'm going to go into my own history here as a case in point, so that you might feel comfortable to start delving in to your own relationship with food to get a sense of what might be stopping you from making the changes you need to make to be well. Whenever I look at the question of mindset I like to pay homage to Albert Einstein who said something that is at the same time both very whimsical and very profound. What he said was that 'Everybody is a genius. But if you judge a fish by it's ability to climb a tree, it will live its life believing that it is stupid.'

I mention this here because from as far back as I can remember up until I got a handle on things at the ripe old age of 52 when I wrote *Thrive in Midlife*, my relationship with food had been a very problematic one. I now know after years of therapy and wellness retreats that this came out of entrenched beliefs that I'd developed early in life about my worthiness. To cut a long story short, with these beliefs underlying my conscious and unconscious thought patterns, I developed a number of dangerous strategies that enabled me to wrap my life around the crippling body image issues that came with my ideas about worthiness in general, and what it meant to be a woman in particular.

The bottom line is that my build does not lend itself to the kind of willowy long legged super-thin look made popular by the models I used to see in magazines like Cleo and Dolly when I was a highly impressionable young girl. In fact, I was about 12 when I decided that I was going to do whatever it took to look like those models. This is when I started to be a fish who was trying to climb a tree as Einstein would say. The awful thing is that I'm by no means the only person to be affected in this way. In fact, there's an epidemic of this kind of thing out there right now that cuts across socio economic, age, geographic, and to some extent gender boundaries as well. For my own part I can say that my ideas about where I sat in the world led me to some really wild and crazy behaviour around food over the ensuing decades. The whole catastrophe saw my weight go up and down like a proverbial yoyo, and definitely did my body no good at all from either a short or a long-term perspective.

It makes me sad to think that I was barely in double digits when I started relating to food in a way that was diagnosed as binge eating disorder several decades later. I'm actually grateful to menopause for forcing me into a place where I finally had to get out of my head and into my body, and get real with myself about the damage I was doing to my body and my soul. It was only a couple of years ago, that I learnt how to use mindfulness to tap into my brain's neuroplasticity to rewire old patterns whenever I noticed that I was being triggered in a way that made me vulnerable to relapsing into negative thoughts and behaviours around food. This is when I was able to really start turning my life around. Over time I got really good at pausing and feeling into my body to interrupt any old patterns that might otherwise play out particularly when I'm stressed, upset, tired or even just bored. Mindfulness works because it firmly anchors us in the here and now. This is important because the here and now is the only place we can take action, and therefore the only place where we can affect our outcomes. The flip side is that living in a world of magical tomorrows, or being stuck in the past will ultimately undermine our ability to change and be well.

What we need to do is strip everything right back and remember that the point of eating is to provide our bodies with the nutrients it needs to survive. So how is it then that the world is facing an epidemic of obesity and preventable disease associated with eating the wrong kinds of foods? As I see it, essentially there are two interrelated forces at play here. First and foremost is mindset, which I hope you can now see is something you can turn around in your favour. And then there is the question of the way the food and diet industries manipulate us to achieve the corporate goals of the multinational companies that dominate them. The more I delved in to what was actually in many of the apparently harmless foods that are marketed to us as being healthy when I was doing my research for *Thrive in Midlife*, the more I realized that there are probably a lot of people who are unwittingly compromising their quality of life in general by replacing whole foods with processed foods because they think they are healthy. The awful thing is about these foods is not only that they are not healthy, but that they are also addictive.

On a psychological level when I had no awareness whatsoever of the way addictions work, it felt like there was a bully in my head who would hound me to get skinnier and skinnier, whilst there was also a mad woman who was trying to fill the gap in her heart by eating her way into numbness.

It's only relatively recently that I've been able to coach people around their issues with food. Early on in my coaching career I had way too many triggers to have been of any use to anyone wanting to delve into this area. These days when I sit down with clients who've got issues around body image and/or eating, I guide them to get present in their bodies, and to recognize whether they're using any of the three key strategies we often unconsciously use to keep ourselves stuck.

These three strategies are blame, justification, and denial. I know that I unconsciously used all of these in a big way over the decades that I lost to obsessing over my weight. I can still remember thinking things like, 'It's not fair, it's not my fault, I inherited a sweet tooth and a stodgy metabolism from my mother and an addictive gene from my father'.

This is an example of blame. There's, 'I'll start eating well and exercising tomorrow. I've got too much on today'. This is an example of justification. And there's, 'I'm not too bad really. Sure, I might be a complete couch potato and eat way too much crap, but I don't drink or smoke and I'm going to eat perfectly and exercise my butt off every day for the rest of my life from tomorrow'. This one is an example of denial. Strategies like these keep us stuck because they distract us from taking responsibility for our behaviour and its effect on our wellbeing. In my own case when I nutted out the program I put myself through for *Thrive in Midlife* it just became too hard for me to maintain the sorts of stories I used to spin to myself, once I became conscious of how they were keeping me stuck, and once I learnt how to feel into my body for clues about what was really going on when I felt like things going awry. Now I didn't master this overnight of course, but over time I got better and better at catching myself on the brink of a binge and reminding myself that the fundamental reason we eat is to fuel our body up so that it can function well. It isn't to stem boredom. It isn't to reward ourselves. It isn't to punish ourselves. And it isn't to numb our feelings. Numbing my feelings was a big one back in the day. Once I recognised what was going on, I was able to go in to what was behind the need to binge and thereby get numb, and then go about addressing that need in a more healthful way. For me bingeing was a way to avoid my feelings. Relearning how to be comfortable actually feeling my feelings was a big part of the puzzle that I needed to put together so that I could break free of my dysfunctional relationship with food for once and for all.

I know that not everyone who wants to lose weight got into the position they're in because of a dysfunctional relationship with food. But whatever's going on for you, taking the time to look under the hood to see how you're positioned in terms of your mindset on a day to day basis will go a long way to bringing you back to a place where you're not wasting time on mindless thoughts and actions that can spiral out of control into obsessions or addictions if they're left unchecked. When I wrote *Thrive in Midlife* I developed a number of strategies that were effective in getting centred and grounded in order to weather the storm of menopause better than I might otherwise have done. These are the very same strategies that I used again when I got into the initial particularly challenging phase of the Sirtfood protocol.

The thing to be aware of is that it's very easy to default to old patterns of thinking until you really solidify your new more healthful patterns. What you need to do is be patient and persistent in establishing the new patterns that are ultimately going to get you to where you want to be. If you think about the fact that you've been wiring the old patterns into your brain if not for your whole life, then at least for a significant chunk of it, then it's not hard to see that there's a considerable act of will required to reprogram yourself for success in relation to your health goals.

I talked earlier about the belief I developed early on in my life about worthiness. I wonder if that resonated with you at all? The bottom line is that you don't have to do too much research to see that there's an epidemic of body image issues fuelled by negative thinking going on out there. As Brené Brown says in her wonderful book, *Daring Greatly*, "after all of the consciousness raising and critical awareness, we still feel the most shame about not being thin, young, and beautiful enough." Brené Brown is renowned for her work on shame and vulnerability. I want you to pause for a moment and think about the extent to which avoiding vulnerability might have limited your ability to be really happy and well in the past, and how albeit unconscious shame of some kind or other might have stopped you from seeing all of the ways in which you are, in the sense that Brene Brown brings to the table, 'good enough'. The exercises at the end of this chapter invite you to look at these kinds of questions and hopefully get an experience of what it's like to not be hampered by the sort of negative beliefs that predispose us to only see the ways in which we are 'not good enough'. In my own case, my disordered thinking around food was locked in with my disordered thinking about my self worth for several decades. It makes me really sad to think that some people actually take this kind of thinking to the grave with them. I don't want you to be one of those people.

This seems like a good time to remind you about Albert Einstein's quote about the fish and the tree again. As Brené Brown notes, "women generally tend to include judgments about themselves based on the way they look at least as much as what they've achieved, how they feel, or who they are". My mission is to help women to stop being a fish climbing a tree because of buying in to the artificial images of women we see plastered on magazine covers, in the movies, and in advertisements for clothes, beauty products and anything promoting the idea of what it is to be successful. I want you to think about what the sensationalised photos of celebrities who've put on weight, or dared to go outside without their makeup on, or who've been dumped by their celebrity husband for a younger version of themselves is doing to our collective consciousness. And from your own perspective, consider the way that these things have subtly and covertly reinforced your more or less well entrenched inferiority complex, and shamed you into submission when your defences were down.

Writing *Thrive in Midlife* forced me to unpack my stuff to the extent that I was able to catch a glimpse of who I really was without the veil of the 'not good enough' worldview draped over me. I'm now driven to help other women avoid spending their life being distracted by how much they weigh, how much body fat they have, and what they see when they look in the mirror with the kind of nasty critical gaze that the world we live in can make us think is our own. It's all about building emotional and physical resilience, and adopting a vocabulary that reinforces all of the ways in which we are not only good enough, but in fact fantastic.

Doing the work to get clear on this stuff is really important because if body image issues are left unchecked, they will almost certainly intensify as we experience the changes that come about as we age. Let's just agree that worrying about being a fish who can't climb a tree is an exercise in futility and a license to be miserable. With effort and focus, I was able to swap that kind of license for one that cleared the way for me to be, for the most part, happy and well. The strategies I'm including in this book will help you do that too. You will literally breathe life into your future like I did. Among other things it's all about working with, rather than against, the biological changes that getting older brings with it. The clock doesn't stand still for anyone, but we can certainly slow it down with wise lifestyle choices around what we eat, think, and do.

If you don't take the initiative to manage what goes on in your mind, you'll find that your mind manages you with its default programs. One of these involves compulsively thinking. Another one adds automatic negative thoughts that seem to spring up out of nowhere into the mix. I'm sure you know what these are. They're the 'not good enough' scripts that might be phrased in terms of not being thin enough, smart enough, blonde enough, tall enough, popular enough, rich enough, young enough, etc. And by the way, these work just as effectively for men as they do for women. It's just that they might be worded differently for men to include things like not being virile enough, ripped enough, successful enough, etc.

In addition to the ideas around blame, justification, and denial that I mentioned earlier, we can add 'generalising' and 'perfectionism' in as a couple more of the corrosive frameworks that can keep us cycling around our problems without making any ground in terms of transcending them. Brené Brown's take on perfectionism is that rather than it driving us toward being better, it's actually just shame wearing a disguise that ultimately keeps us small. 'Not good enough' is the language of shame that leaves us feeling as if there's something terribly wrong with us at our core. Generalising takes something like - 'I'm not good enough', and turns it into something like - 'I'll never be good enough' or 'I'm no good at anything'. You take your power back if you can catch yourself whenever you notice that you're thinking like this, and deliberately rewrite the script to reflect the degree of respect and esteem that you know deep down that you deserve.

Another thing that keeps us stuck is compulsively doing, rather than being. Being busy involves going here, going there, doing this and doing that. Never slowing down to feel, and to check in with our body to find out what's real. Starting to experience life on the level of feeling rather than just on the level of thinking was a real game changer for me. It became all about more pausing and feeling into my body for clues about what was really going on, and less thinking and running around without any sense of my body in space or time whatsoever.

We look at stress in some detail in the next chapter, but for now I just want to acknowledge that it's the mind that keeps us stressed. It's never the circumstances of our life, but rather our thoughts and reactions to them that lead to stress building up in our bodies. The thing is that our body knows how to relax, and I've provided some exercises at the end of this chapter that are all about creating the conditions for you to feel into your body to short-circuit the programming that might otherwise play out in your mind with the negative side effect of keeping your body stressed.

There's absolutely no one-size fits all proposition here. This chapter is all about getting you to think about exactly what's going to work best for you to help you to easefully arrive at a healthy weight. I know I just talked about thinking less and feeling more, but you'll approach your thoughts differently as you get into the swing of being mindful, and start asking yourself the kinds of questions that will open you up to your body, your soul, and your heart, rather than keeping you confined to the space between your ears. You'll need to make a commitment to set some quality time aside where you won't be disturbed to work your way through the questions in the following exercises at a deep level. I want you to, among other things, set an intention to create a metaphorical soft place to fall if you ever need one. You can keep this handy moving forward into a life that won't have you continually bumping into hard surfaces in your mind all of the time. Turning this corner in your life is about what Brené Brown says involves, "taking the long journey from what people think, to deeply believing that you are enough".

FLUSHING OUT EXERCISE

This exercise will enable you to take a snapshot of the tone of your current mindset. To prepare for this exercise, it's best to sit comfortably and take a couple of nice long, deep breaths. Notice any tension in your body. Then notice what happens to that tension as you ask yourself the following questions:

- Where am I applying perfectionism in my life?

_____

_____

_____

_____

- How do I feel about that aspect of my life right now?

_____

_____

_____

_____

- In what ways am I doing well in this aspect of my life right now?

_____

_____

_____

_____

- In which other areas of my life am I doing really well?

  _____
  _____
  _____
  _____

- What drains my energy?

  _____
  _____
  _____
  _____

- What could I do to limit this drainage?

  _____
  _____
  _____
  _____

- How do I show myself respect?

  _____
  _____
  _____
  _____

- How else could I show myself respect?

_____
_____
_____
_____

- How easy or hard have I made it to feel good?

_____
_____
_____
_____

- What could I do to make it easier to feel good?

_____
_____
_____
_____

- Is blame, justification, denial, perfectionism or any other thought process stopping me from taking care of my health?

_____
_____
_____
_____

- What strategies will I put in place to avoid being stopped or slowed down by thought processes like the ones above?

___

- What is being stopped or slowed down by thought processes like the ones above, and what have they cost me so far in my life?

___

- What could I replace this behavior with?

___

- What do I say to myself when I look in the mirror?

  _____
  _____
  _____
  _____

- What's a more empowering thing I could say?

  _____
  _____
  _____
  _____

- What things could I do to cultivate more self-compassion?

  _____
  _____
  _____
  _____

Sit quietly now and consider what your answers to these questions mean in relation to your health goals, and note down any strategies you'd like to follow through with that emerged from this exercise.

SELF-COMPASSION REPAIR KIT

The list below includes the qualities I recognised that I needed, to cultivate more self-compassion. You might like to add or delete anything so that the list resonates with you. So, for me to cultivate more self-compassion I needed to develop:

- The ability to forgive myself for only doing the best I could in the past, present, and future.
- The ability to forgive the other people in my life for only doing the best they could in the past, present, and future.
- The permission to ask for help when I need it.
- The willingness to give myself permission to be well, happy, and grounded.
- The awareness to know when I'm numbing my feelings, and the strength to stop doing it.
- The awareness and generosity to recognise and celebrate my wins.
- The generosity to cut myself some slack when I make a mistake.
- The courage to take life as it comes and stop trying to plan and control everything.
- The wisdom and the strength to lean into discomfort.
- The generosity to stop caring what other people think about me.
- The wisdom to stop comparing myself to others.
- The ability to feel my feelings and above all else, the ability and willingness to receive and give love wholeheartedly.

THE HERO'S JOURNEY PERSPECTIVE EXERCISE

The framework of the Hero's Journey came out of Joseph Campbell's fascination with mythology. His signature work *The Hero with a Thousand Faces* elaborates on the core idea that stories, and beyond that in fact, our whole life, plays out in terms of patterns within what he calls the monomyth. I find this to be a very helpful framework to consider challenges within. Before answering the questions below, I want you to watch a video or two on YouTube about the Hero's Journey.

https://www.youtube.com/watch?v=Hhk4N9A0oCA
https://www.youtube.com/watch?v=KGV1BvnyvGo

Whether you choose to go with my favourites or find another one you like, I'd like you to watch it with your weight loss journey in mind. Once you've watched one or more of these videos, I want you to consider the following questions:

- Describe who you are in the ordinary world?
- What does it feel like to be you?
- How do you feel about the idea of doing what it takes to reach your ideal weight?

Thinking of yourself as having answered the call to adventure in relation to taking care of yourself in respect of your weight;

- Consider what caused you to answer the call?
- What will it cost you if you do not follow through?

- On a scale of 1 to 10, how confident are you about reaching your health goals?

Thinking of the threshold you are about to pass through in answering the call:

- What obstacles are you likely to encounter?
- What resources will you call on to overcome these obstacles?
- What allies are likely to turn up for you?

Thinking of returning to the ordinary world:

- What will be different about you?
- What will be different for you?
- What opportunities will you take advantage of?
- On a sale of 1 to 10, how likely you are to get to your ideal weight in the next 12 months?

I want to wish you huge success in relation to developing a mindset that supports you to achieve your goals in relation to your weight, your health, and your life in general. I also want to remind you to be in touch with me if you ever want a hand with any of this material. As I mentioned in the introduction, this is a Hero's Journey. Heroes don't become heroes by going it alone the whole way. They know when to enlist help. I invite you to stay tuned into your own needs through your Hero's Journey, and never shy away from calling in your allies when the time is right.

94

CHAPTER FIVE

The Sleep Factor

The time when we're asleep is the time when our body gets on with the healing and repair work it needs to do to keep us well. Among other things, good quality sleep is critical for maintaining a healthy balance of the hormones that drive all of the core processes in our body. Also when we don't get enough sleep, our levels of ghrelin, the hormone that makes us feel hungry goes up, and our levels of leptin, the hormone that helps us feel full goes down. This explains why we seem to put on weight when we're sleep deprived. Sure, we have willpower to rely on, but my own and more recently my clients' experience of this territory adds weight to the theory that willpower only works in the short term because our reserves of willpower deplete if we are forced to resist temptation after temptation ongoingly.

And if all of that's not bad enough, not getting enough sleep also affects how our body reacts to insulin. Real difficulties arise when we're struggling with a sleep deficit leading to higher than normal blood sugar levels because this condition alters the way our brain and body respond to glucose. All of this leaves our system under-fuelled and over-stressed, which leads to physical, mental, and emotional exhaustion. And this is the state that sets our body up to desperately seek energy with the classic sugar and caffeine cravings that I'm sure you're all more or less familiar with. I know I am.

According to a report commissioned by the Sleep Health Foundation in 2011, almost 9% of the adult population in Australia or some 1.5 million people suffer from sleep disorders. This equated at the time to a staggering $818 million in costs to the health system from sleep disorders and the plethora of conditions stemming from a lack of good quality sleep.

This question of our ability to get a good night's sleep matters not only because everything looks and feels better when we've slept well, but our health overall relies on it. I described the fallout from the heat filled sleepless nights that I used to regularly experience when hot flushes were an ongoing occurrence for me in *Thrive in Midlife*. I had sheets and bedding strewn all over the place, and books and magazines spread over the bed and the floor around it. Basically, the room looked like a war zone with all of the things I'd grabbed through the night to try to get my mind off the overwhelm and desperation that I would inevitably succumb to as a result of not being able to get to sleep. When I looked in the mirror in the morning I just looked and felt like I was way past my use by date. And little did I know at the time, that the weight I was stacking on was due in part to the way my body was reacting to the kind of sleep deficit I was racking up.

I'm going to really drive this point home, because we're up against a culture that almost promotes working more and sleeping less. In her book *Thrive*, Arianna Huffington mentions a dinner party she was at where a man bragged to her about only getting four hours of sleep the night before. She then went on to say that she "resisted the temptation to tell him that the dinner would have been a lot more interesting if he had gotten five". She also mentioned that Bill Clinton, who was well known to short change himself in relation to sleep, told her that "every important mistake I've made in my life, I've made because I was too tired." For my own part, I'm pretty much over the messages the world continually gives us in one form or other that equates being busy with being successful. Back in 2014 whether it was due to the effect of hot flushes, or a lack of ability to wind down at the end of the day because of the ridiculously packed schedule I had, the fact was that I was starting to rack up a sleep deficit that was seriously eroding my quality of life. This ultimately led me to the edge of burnout which made it even harder for me to get my head around what I needed to do to stay mentally, financially, and physically fit, in light of the fact that I was facing redundancy at the time as well as the onset of menopause at exactly the same time as my daughter was going into adolescence. Before too long it became obvious to me that this question of sleep was one of the key areas I needed to work on to get my life back on track to make sure that the whole sorry mess didn't come tumbling down on top of me. Not to mention being able to manage my weight more effectively. There was a real chicken and egg scenario at play here too, because not only does sleeping well enable our body to manage our weight better, but also eating well in general and getting processed foods in particular out of our life helps to promote better sleep as well.

And the list of reasons to establish good sleeping patterns goes on. It slows down the aging process. It leads to better access to the prefrontal cortex where good decisions and willpower arise from, and it leads to more human growth hormone or HGH being released into our body as well. And believe me you don't want to short change yourself in this regard in midlife in particular, because HGH is responsible for stimulating the regeneration of cells and the burning of fat, along with the building of muscle, and the stimulation of the immune system.

Fluctuating and, in particular, declining levels of hormones like estrogen and progesterone can lead to sleep disorders in women who've never had them before. Along with causing hot flushes and contributing to irritability, declining levels of estrogen also slows down the body's intake and production of magnesium, which helps our muscles to relax and thereby makes it easier to get to sleep. So, whether the case of your difficulties with sleep stem back to hormonal fluctuations or something else entirely, it's worth getting to the bottom of the problem because good quality sleep is critical for our mental health, our physical health, our quality of life, and our safety. I threw the point about safety in here because the risk of accidents of all kinds is increased when we operate in the zombie-like state we wind up in when we're sleep deprived. As mentioned above, the cost of sleep deprivation to Australia's economy is significant, and this is mirrored in the US where the National Centre on Sleep Disorders Research estimates that the cost of sleep disorders, sleep deprivation, and sleepiness, is almost sixteen million dollars in direct costs, and fifty to a hundred billion a year in indirect costs such as accidents.

What's less well known is that being tired makes it very difficult for us to tap into our reserves of willpower that we need to make sure that any of our plans to maintain a healthy lifestyle don't go out the window at the first scent of freshly baked muffins coming out of the local Baker's Delight store or wherever. As Kelly McGonigal says in her great book *The Willpower Instinct*, "even being mildly but chronically sleep deprived makes us more susceptible to stress, cravings, and temptation". It also makes it difficult to control our emotions and to focus our attention, as well as increasing the risk of chronic health problems, like heart disease, kidney disease, high blood pressure, diabetes, stroke, and obesity.

We look at stress in some detail in the next chapter, so all I'll say here is that stress of one kind or other is believed to be one of the main causes of short term sleep difficulties. The other side of the coin is that sleep is important from the point of view of managing stress. So, let's get down to brass tacks now and take a look at what we can do to break this vicious cycle. To start with, one of the most basic things we can do to increase our chances of sleeping well is to lower the level of adrenaline in our body. Adrenaline is one of the stress hormones that triggers the fight or flight response you will hear more about in the next chapter on Stress. When we're feeding our body well, exercising regularly, and relaxing well by meditating and/or practicing mindfulness throughout the day, we're priming our body to sleep more deeply.

There are also seven proactive and really fundamental steps listed below for a good night's sleep that are sometimes referred to as sleep hygiene that I've listed below. The bottom line is that it makes a lot of sense to get into the habit of setting yourself up to sleep well via strategies like these as a fundamental contribution to your ability to manage your weight, and live a full and happy life.

1. Keeping the bedroom quiet, dark, and at a comfortable temperature.
2. Not having a big meal and avoiding caffeine and alcohol for at least 3 hours before going to bed.
3. Exercising regularly but not within 3 hours of bedtime.
4. Doing whatever you need to do to relax before going to bed, such as taking a bath, reading a book, and above all avoid using screen based devices at least 1 hour before bedtime.
5. Keeping the bedroom for sleeping and intimacy, rather than using it as a part time office or grievance raising arena.
6. Getting up at the same time every day.
7. Getting adequate levels of sunshine to boost your melatonin and serotonin, which are the hormones that get us into the rhythm of sleeping and waking.

CHAPTER SIX

The Stress Factor

Picture a scenario like this. You're having problems at work. You're running around like a mad thing day in and day out, catering to the needs of others without a moment to yourself, and to make matters worse your clothes are starting to feel really tight because you've started eating way too much comfort food as well. It might not be the first thing you think of, but it's highly likely that stress is one of the main culprits in the weight gain aspect of this scenario. This is because just as a lack of sleep makes it harder to maintain a healthy weight, stress sets you up to struggle in this regard as well.

The fact of the matter is that most of us become vulnerable to overeating when we're feeling stressed. This happens thanks to our body's natural stress response that sets off a number of physiological changes whenever it gets activated. One of these is that our sympathetic nervous system becomes dominant. It's our sympathetic nervous system that gives rise to the classic fight or flight scenario that we equate with being stressed, whilst it's the parasympathetic nervous system that we want to spend most of our time in because it slows everything down and allows our body to get on with its growth and repair work that's put on the backburner when the sympathetic nervous system is switched on.

This is why it's important to manage the stress we experience on a day to day basis that all too often takes us away from that quiet, still place of calm that we've all got at our core. Many of us go so far down the tunnel of stress that it feels like there's no way back. But there is a way back. It involves unlearning the things that we've learnt throughout our lives that disconnect us from our core.

It took me years to learn to get out of my head and into my body which is the key to getting a handle on the level of stress we expose ourselves to. So don't be too hard on yourself if this doesn't feel natural at first. It's actually the most natural thing in the world, but there's a bit of gentle reprogramming involved in undoing the patterns that have set your sympathetic nervous system up as your default state. The process of turning this around and soothing yourself so that your parasympathetic nervous system is reset as your default is like peeling back the layers of an onion. Each time you work on this you'll gradually feel yourself building the bridge back to your central place of calm. It's all about being more and more able to be fully present and grounded in the here and now.

Bringing this shift into your day to day state is a matter of going right back to the fundamentals of breathing and pausing. This is because what mindfully pausing regularly throughout the day does for us on a physical level, is to re-engage our parasympathetic nervous system.

One of the surprising things to know about stress is that it takes us out of our prefrontal cortex. This is the most recently evolved part of our brain that's responsible for things like reasoning and decision-making. Stress kicks us back into our brain's limbic system. This is where we're operating from when we experience the fight, flight or freeze behaviour that characterises the stress response. It's interesting for me to look back on the time just before I started writing *Thrive in Midlife*. As I mentioned earlier, bingeing was a strategy I used to numb my feelings of vulnerability at that time. I'd been strengthening the neural networks that went from fear and other negative emotions straight to highly processed sweet and fatty foods for decades before that. My behaviour around food well and truly screwed my body's reward system up. This meant that I was really behind the eight ball in terms of dopamine spiking in my body at the worst time possible in terms of losing weight and maintaining any success I managed to have in this regard. The point is that like everyone else I'm vulnerable to defaulting to old unhealthy patterns of behaviour when I'm stressed. The kicker is that one of the biggest stressors in my life at that time was my eating disorder, with the aftermath of a binge resulting in feelings of hopelessness, guilt, shame, and disgust.

Even now when I'm a full two years away from playing out unhealthy behaviour around food, I still know that I'm never more than one decision away from falling off the wagon. And without a doubt I can say that when I'm stressed is when I'm most vulnerable in this regard. To be honest I can't really be sure at this stage whether I'll ever be completely free and clear. That's why I'm such an advocate for managing stress these days.

Even without the added stress someone who doesn't eat well puts on their digestive and other systems, stress is terrible from the point of view of our gut health. Digesting food well is not one of the things our limbic system cares about. Evolution gave us a stress response so that we can run or fight to save our lives in the event of real and present danger. The problem is that priming our body to do that comes at the expense of our digestive system's ability to extract nutrition from the food we eat and eliminate the toxins that are released in the process. Because of this and other aspects of what goes on when the sympathetic nervous system is running the show, we can see that stress speeds up the aging process, as well as increasing our chance of developing heart disease, diabetes, and depression.

This is because switching on the sympathetic nervous system raises our blood sugar and heart rate, and narrows our blood vessels. This is what's behind our heart madly pumping blood to our head, our lungs, and the muscles in our legs and arms to get energy to where it's needed as fast as possible in the event of danger. Meanwhile the immune system is also activated to enhance our blood clotting capability and blunt our pain perception. Again, these things are helpful in an emergency, but very unhelpful from the point of view of our overall health if they become the norm rather than the exception.

As I mentioned above, the body also automatically switches off any non-essential activity that could drain the energy stores that are needed to survive the dangerous environment it perceives that we're in. In addition to digestion that I mentioned above, these non-essential activities include things like growth and repair, reproduction, and higher order cognitive activities like reasoning, decision making, and willpower. Of course, there are obvious problems with this given the chronically high levels of stress many people live with these days. You simply don't want energy being diverted away from these processes indefinitely. The point of this highly effective basic survival system that evolved millions of years ago, is to be used in the event of real danger. It's not meant to be switched on the whole time because we're running late for a meeting, or we can't find our car keys, or whatever. And it's not meant to be switched on and off continually either.

Things changed for me in relation to stress in 2014 when I realised that as well as circumstances, things like thoughts, memories and emotions are also triggers for stress, and regardless of what's going on in relation to the circumstances in our life, it's the big negative emotions like shame, anger, and fear that are likely to be playing in the back of our mind when we're tossing and turning in bed in the middle of the night.
I included the exercises in the previous chapter because when we consider what's actually happening to the body when we push the stress button, it's obvious that we need to get a handle on things if we want to live to a ripe, old age at a healthy weight, and avoid the preventable diseases that stressing too much and carrying too much weight can predispose us to. It's because the parasympathetic nervous system is inhibited during the stress response that we're not able to benefit from its ability to calm our body down. This is where things like meditation

and mindfulness really come into their own. They are incredibly effective at brining us back to the state where our parasympathetic nervous system is dominant. The parasympathetic nervous system basically does exactly the opposite of what the sympathetic nervous system does. It creates the ideal conditions for routine activities like digestion, growth, and repair to take place. It slows our heart rate, and lowers our blood pressure. Breathing and pausing is the way to reengage the parasympathetic nervous system.

On the other hand, the sympathetic nervous system floods the body with adrenaline which increases blood flow and cortisol, whose primary function is to increase blood sugar to get energy to the parts of the body that need it in an emergency. The problem here from the point of view of our weight is that cortisol relies on an enzyme found in fat tissue to increase blood sugar. The consequence of this is that the stress response sends a message to our body to lay down fat stores so that we have the energy within them when we need it.

Furthermore, not only are we likely to put on weight when we're stressed, but we're also activating inflammation because of the process going on to mobilise sugar for energy. The kicker is that inflammation adds an additional layer of physical stress for the body to handle as well. So this is a vicious cycle that I really want to support you to empower yourself to get out of.

The problem is that many of us lead lives that mean we're chronically experiencing increased blood pressure, which leads to hypertension. Chronic hypertension sets us up for damage to our blood vessels, and what's worse, when the metabolic stress response and the cardiac stress response intersect, plaque is likely to start to form in our blood vessels. The mobilisation of the fats lead to scarring of the blood vessels via the force and volume of the blood being pumped around the body under stress, and there's a real risk that if the plaques in the vessels break off they could travel to the brain in the case of a stroke, or the heart in the case of a heart attack.

What many people experience in their day-to-day existence is a series of mini stress events. The consequence of this is that firstly the stress response results in the fat cells releasing energy, then when the danger or perceived danger has passed fat gets stored back in the cells in the complex form that it started out in, and so on and so forth. All of this activity is definitely not what the body wants in terms of homeostasis. The bottom line is that chronic stress makes the control of sugar more difficult. This matters because we risk developing insulin resistance when we've consistently got too much sugar in our bloodstream, and insulin resistance is the precursor to type 2 diabetes. As far as I'm concerned, type 2 diabetes is the canary in the coalmine in terms of the modern western diet coupled with the levels of stress that many of us live with.

I'll mention willpower again here, because if I haven't already flagged enough reasons for you to commit to working out how to manage your stress yet, there's also the fact that stress makes it almost impossible to draw on the willpower instinct that you're going to be needing to access to resist the urge to comfort eat. This is because you need to be operating from your prefrontal cortex to access your willpower instinct, and you're stuck in your brain's limbic system when you're stressed.

There's no executive decision making going on when you're in the stress response, and your ability to maintain a healthy perspective on things goes out the window as well. Living with chronic stress is like swimming in a rip in the ocean. We're culturally programmed to value action and being busy, but action in a rip equates to struggle, and the struggle will wear you out eventually. On the other hand, if you dive under all of the activity by breathing deeply and bringing yourself into the present moment, you'll sense a point when you can still yourself and feel into your core. That is the point where you can make it to calmer waters where among other things you can make sensible decisions about what to eat, and all of the other lifestyle factors that add up to the difference between a happy and healthy future, or a miserable future filled with pain and illness.

Stress also plays a major role in depression. Women are twice as likely to suffer from depression as men. And there are particular life phases when women are more likely to have an episode of depression than others, with puberty, menopause and the postnatal period being the obvious hot spots.

The bottom line is that taking control of your stress will enable you to experience better sleep, as well as having better access to your willpower instinct and the other faculties that come with a well functioning prefrontal cortex. Not only will you be less likely to develop depression, but you'll have better digestion, and better health overall.

Many of the strategies in this book will set you up to be spending a lot less time with your sympathetic nervous system switched on. Eating in a way that supports your body, exercising, sleeping well, and having a healthier mindset, are all going to predispose you to being calmer and happier. And the mental decluttering exercise at the end of this chapter will help you to take a lot of the material with heavy energy wrapped around it off your mind as well.

The one thing that's always available to us and that has an almost immediate effect on dampening down stress is mindful breathing. When we're relaxed, we tend to breathe slowly and deeply, rather than taking quick shallow breaths that are the hallmark of stress. Deliberately making time to pause between activities and just breathing deeply will make a much bigger difference to your overall health than you can probably imagine at the moment if you're reading this book in the middle of a stressful day. Simply focusing on your breath and slowing it down sets up a feedback mechanism that tells your body that everything's okay. That way it knows that it doesn't have to be on standby for an emergency with the sympathetic nervous system engaged or semi engaged all of the time.

Whilst stress is well known as the fight and flight response, the fact that relaxation creates a kind of pause and plan response is less well known. Suzan Segerstrom from the University of Kentucky, School of Psychology, coined this phrase. So, what I'm suggesting here is that you plan to pause regularly throughout the day. In the beginning, you'll need to get very deliberate about this until it becomes second nature to you. The strategies in this chapter are aimed at helping you to keep things in perspective. Basically, they'll set you up to be less reactive to the waxing and waning of your emotions, and the spiking of energy around you. Life will always throw up challenges. It's up to us how we choose to respond to them. This explains why exactly the same event will cause one person's stress levels to go through the roof and another person's to hardly be affected at all. It's the intersection of our biology, our psychology, our circumstances and our coping mechanisms that explain this kind of phenomenon.

Breathing mindfully, journaling, meditating, and talking over our concerns with friends, are all examples of effective coping strategies that I urge you to cultivate. What I call regularly de-cluttering your mind is another coping strategy that is going to make a difference to your ability to manage your stress as well.

Before I get you to do the Mind De-Cluttering Exercise over the page, I'll leave you to ponder the conclusions of a study coming out of the University of California where it was found that "the more a group of stressed-out, overweight women meditated, the greater the decrease in their anxiety, chronic stress and belly fat – without any diet changes." Is it worth learning to meditate and calm your system down? I think so.

MIND DECLUTTERING EXERCISE

On the following page, I want you to write down everything that's on your mind at the moment. Give yourself as long as you need, and when you think you've finished ask yourself 'what else'? You want to make sure that you get everything out of your head and on to the page. Whether it's about booking yourself in to see your dentist, or calling a friend you haven't seen for a while. Whether it's a nagging concern about getting fat or dying young, or whatever. Get it all down on paper. You might be surprised to see what's been lurking in the back of your mind. This is one of those classic energy drainers you hopefully flushed out in the Flushing Out Exercise.

Once you've got your list ready, I want you to turn to the next page and list out the things you can't do anything about.

Then I want you to go to the next page after that and list out the things you can do something about.

When you've finished your list of things you can do something about, I want you to schedule any key activities that you need to undertake to resolve or progress these matters into your diary. Now we all know things might get in the way in terms of getting everything we schedule in our diary done by exactly the date we planned to have it done by. But the point of this exercise is for you to literally take a load off your mind. What's more, you'll also eventually unearth issues around things in your diary that have emotional baggage and/or unrealistic expectations linked to them, as well as any patterns of self-sabotage that are playing out in your life. A red flag goes up on anything that is continually shunted along from week to week without any progress being made whatsoever. You might like to call on help to investigate what's going on in the event of issues remaining unresolved for extended periods without any valid reason.

Last but not least, I want you to take the page of things you can't do anything about and write on it with a big texta; 'concern noted' before filing it at the end of your diary for review further down the track. If you feel like it, you could even flush it down the toilet, or burn it, or just put it in the bin. This doesn't mean that the points on it are not important, it just means you don't need to have these things playing on your mind in the way they have been to date.

WHAT'S ON MY MIND

THINGS I CAN'T DO ANYTHING ABOUT

THINGS I CAN DO SOMETHING ABOUT

FOUR DAILY RITUALS

These rituals are designed to enable you to improve your ability to remain positive, energised, focussed, and relaxed.

1. Three Relaxing Minutes:

Every night before you go to bed:

- Sit comfortably with a pad and pen nearby. Close your eyes, breathe deeply without forcing anything, and just feel into your body. Notice any thoughts, feelings, emotions, worries, sounds, smells or other sensations that arise. Don't engage with them or try to suppress or change them in any way. Just observe them.
- Maintain this practice for three minutes.
- Then open your eyes and notice your body supported in the chair. Notice what you can see, smell and hear. Wriggle your toes and stretch your arms above your head to ground yourself in the here and now.
- Now take the pad and pen and write down:
    - Any ideas or feelings that came up during this exercise.
    - At least one thing about yourself that you like.
    - At least one thing you did well today.
    - At least one thing that you feel grateful for.

2. Three Grounding Minutes:

On waking every morning:

- Spend a moment to remember what you're grateful for. Just sit with the felt sense of this gratitude in your body for 3 minutes. Allow yourself to bask in the glow of that feeling. Again, just observe any thoughts that cross your mind without feeling that you need to do anything about them.

- Set your intention about what you plan to achieve today and what you need to do to achieve this (specifically in relation to your health goals). Write this down on one or more on post-it notes and stick these wherever you'll be able to see them during the day. Make a point of reviewing your progress at least 3 times during the day. Remember to acknowledge yourself for getting these things done, and reschedule anything that isn't completed.

3. Three Focused Minutes:

Somewhere around the middle of the day:

- Sit quietly with your eyes shut and sense your body working beautifully. Just sit with that felt sense. If there's only one place in your body that feels good on a particular day, feel into it.
- During this time, say to yourself in your mind 'I have everything that I need to achieve my ideal weight', and/or anything else that needs to be said, eg 'I am enough', or 'I am happy, healthy, and strong'. Repeat this 'mantra' for the duration of the practice.
- Notice if you're holding on to any tension in your body. Just breathe into that place and notice the breath enveloping the tension until it dissipates.
- After 3 minutes, bring your attention back into the room by wriggling your toes or whatever works for you, and if there is any unresolved tension, ask yourself what needs to happen for this tension to be released? Sit with this question until the answer comes, or until the tension dissipates.
- After a while if nothing has changed ask, 'Am I prepared to let this tension go?' If nothing comes up for you just ask, 'What needs to happen for me to be ready to let this go?'
- Repeat this until you get an answer, or until you feel like it's time to stop. Sometimes things like this are automatically processed overnight once you shift the energy around them by bringing them into awareness.

4. Daylong Mindfulness:

Whenever you notice negative thoughts coming up throughout the day:

Ask yourself:

- Where did this thought come from?
- What need, issue or problem does this thought serve?
- What can I do to address that need?
- How does this thought limit me?
- What would a more resourceful thought be?
- What comes up for me when I stop and look at thoughts like these?
- How does this exercise shift the energy around the thought?

CHAPTER SEVEN

The Exercise Factor

If there was a reason to avoid exercise, I've tended to be one of those people who would find it. This used to drive my husband crazy, because he had managed to completely turn his life around with exercise when he was confronted by the degree of physical decline entering his mid-fifties brought along with it. In the end, he not only got fitter, stronger, and happier through exercise, but he also managed to build himself a great new career in the fitness industry as well. For my own part, the penny finally dropped shortly after I started writing *Thrive in Midlife*. Not only was I unable to find reasons not to exercise, but I actually started finding reasons to 'just do it' that I'd never even heard of before. Beyond the more obvious ones like building muscle, and increasing flexibility, and cardiovascular fitness, it also turns out that exercise has an important role to play in managing digestion, cholesterol levels, stress, brain health, and our moods as well.

So if exercise is so good for us, you might ask, then why is it that 25% of adults don't do any exercise at all, and 60% don't get enough to sustain a healthy body? Needless to say, I understand only too well on a personal level how it is that 25% of adults don't do any exercise at all, because even after a period of reform when I was writing *Thrive in Midlife*, I'd more or less slipped right back into my old patterns completely by the time I started writing this book.

Habits of inactivity went back a very long way in my life. My aversion to exercise coincided more or less with the onset of puberty. I guess this is not so surprising given that that was the time when I became particularly uncomfortable in the skin I was in on all fronts. There are no prizes for guessing that this was when I started to develop dysfunctional thinking around food as well. Somewhere in the middle of all of this was the capacity I spoke about earlier, where I seemed to be able to believe that somehow, I could start exercising and generally looking after my body tomorrow in a way that I didn't seem to be able to do today. The beauty of this kind of rationale is that if we're effectively able to shift our focus from the here and now to that magical tomorrow, we'll be able to stay in denial about how bad the things we're doing to ourselves really are.

Just like the history of my relationship with food, the history of my relationship to exercise is full of a million magical tomorrows. It was only when things got really bad that I took stock of exactly what my body needed to be well in light of the menopausal symptoms that had pushed me too far out of my comfort zone for my previously effective thought patterns to hold water anymore.

For me, being revisited by the stiffness in my joints, lack of flexibility, aching muscles, lack of strength, and a residual bone density rating that placed me in the stage just prior to osteoporosis that forced me to get real again when I started writing this book. This condition, which is called osteopenia, signals the early stages of bone loss. Those of you who read *Thrive in Midlife* might remember me saying in the part where I reveal the issue with my bone density that "If that wasn't going to add enough fuel to the fire for me to get off the couch and get active, then

I don't know what was." Well in hindsight I can say that it certainly got me off the couch and engaged in a healthy level of activity for about three months, but then slowly after that I gradually drifted into a pattern of predominant inactivity again.

I feel really disappointed that I eventually let the ground I'd made up in relation to exercise all but slip away when the time came to write *Weight Loss in Midlife*. The problem is that disappointment doesn't help me to get fit, so in the end I just had to suck it up, push through any resistance, and just get moving again. To this end, I got back into a routine of doing a few yoga moves to iron out the kinks in my body when I get up in the morning, and walking as fast as I could for 30 minutes every day for a week so that I got my heart rate up, and I got my head around the fact that I was for real in terms of my determination to make some important changes in my life in relation to physical fitness.

After a week of walking and yoga I started to work with hand weights and a simple muscle building routine that a friend who's in the fitness industry devised for me. I launched into it this time with the understanding that a hundred and one little things done frequently can cancel out infrequent more intense bouts of activity, and vice versa.

What I'm getting at here is that you don't need to push yourself to exhaustion and immense physical pain to get results from exercise. When I was younger I had a couple of short-lived spurts of exercising like this. What I know now is that we just need to make a commitment to consistently and strategically moving our body every day, and before too long we'll find that we start to look and feel much better.

What we need to do to start building up our level of wellness is increase our cardio fitness, our flexibility, and our strength in order to maintain if not increase muscle mass. Following the Sirtfood guidelines that Haddon and Goggin provide us with is also helpful because our siruin genes help us to build muscle as well.

CARDIOVASCULAR FITNESS:

What actually happens when we build up our cardio fitness is that our body becomes more efficient at absorbing oxygen. So, when you put your body under the increased demand of a cardio workout, you're priming it to be able to take in more oxygen with less effort, thus improving your chances of avoiding cardiovascular disease. Cardio training is also highly beneficial from the point of view of cholesterol. It improves the amount of HDL relative to the dangerous LDL levels in the bloodstream. Research reveals that a simple shift from low cardiovascular fitness to moderate cardiovascular fitness can reduce the risk of death due to cardiovascular disease by as much as 50%.

The basics of an effective cardio regime include a warm-up and cool-down phase at either end of the workout phase where you want to be maintaining intensity at between 55% and 90% of your maximum heart rate. You can calculate your basic maximum heart rate by subtracting your age from 220. A cardio regime includes the kind of movement you get with exercise like jogging, cycling, aerobics, power walking and aqua aerobics.

It would be ideal to start with at least three 20-minute sessions and work your way up to three 60-minute sessions a week from there. If 20 minutes seems daunting at first, breaking it down into two 10-minute sessions a day while you build your fitness level up is fine. Basically, aim for whatever is going to get you off the starting blocks and build up from there. Aiming for whatever works for you and stretches you, and that you get some enjoyment from at the same time, increases your chances of establishing a sustainable fitness program that will see you keeping your body fit and active throughout your life.

If you still feel like you're at a bit of a loss about where to start, it would be worth thinking about taking on a personal trainer, even if only for a couple of sessions. That way you can be confident that you're going about things in a way that will deliver you the maximum benefits in terms of fitness, and minimise your chances of injuring yourself in the process. If you haven't already done so, your fitness instructor will ask you to get yourself checked out by your doctor first to make sure that there aren't health issues that should be taken into account in designing your exercise program.

MUSCULAR STRENGTH AND ENDURANCE:
Advice from someone trained in fitness was definitely what I needed when I looked at getting into muscular strength and endurance training

in 2014. Muscular endurance training improves the supply of oxygen to the muscles so that you're able to train for longer before lactic acid builds up, whilst muscular strength training increases the cross section of muscle size and strength as a result of the small tears to the tissues that take place at the cellular level when you train. To maximise these kinds of benefits you need to eat adequate amounts of protein and rest between sessions to let the muscle tears repair themselves. It's actually the tearing and repairing that improves your muscle profile overall.

A basic resistance training schedule that combines both strength and endurance benefits includes one set of 8 to 12 repetitions of 8 to 10 different exercises that work all of the major muscle groups. You could start by using lighter weights with a higher number of repetitions and build the weight up gradually. Basically, what you want to be doing is working at an intensity that brings you to the edge of your ability. In other words, don't make it too easy for yourself, but don't go over the edge by making it too hard either.

With resistance training you could be using your body weight for resistance, or exercise machines, or free weights. It feels great now to know that I've re-established a regime where I'm doing something to build muscle and maintain bone density and strength as I move through the last trimester of my life. Activating my sirtuin genes through eating Sirtfoods is also helping in this regard. It's well known that muscle mass and bone density start to decline as we age, without the kind of commitment I'm now making with Sirtfood and physical activity to stop that from happening. Endurance and strength training is also great from the point of view of increasing our metabolic rate, decreasing our blood pressure, and tipping the balance in favour of healthy cholesterol as well.

FLEXIBILITY:

You'll begin to make improvements in your flexibility with your initial morning yoga routine, but you'll definitely benefit from taking this even further. Again, a personal trainer or yoga teacher will show you the best ways to increase your flexibility and balance even more. This aspect of fitness is really important as we age. Losing mobility and strength is often the tipping point for people in terms of confidence, independence and overall enjoyment of life. Modalities like yoga and pilates work by strategically stretching muscles beyond their original length. Meanwhile you get the added benefit of engaging with your breath to relax your body whilst strengthening it at the same time, so there's a double-edged benefit accruing when you do something like yoga.

I want you to understand that I'm not one of those people with a background in physical activity and healthy habits that they can draw on. I mention this because I can imagine some of you feeling intimidated by the idea of getting up and moving, and I want you to know that I know what that's like. In fact, my old mindset saw me stop and start the 42-day program that I set up for myself to be a guinea pig for *Thrive in Midlife* several times. Finding a way to be fully present with myself when this started to happen back in 2014 enabled me to see that

I had a powerful sabotage pattern running in relation to my health in general, and my physical fitness in particular. The fact that I've let the good habits that I put in place back then fall away recently further reinforces the fact that there's more work for me to do in this regard. So, this time around I've made a gilt-edged commitment to myself to make sure that I'm fully present whenever I make decisions that affect my health, especially when it comes to whether I exercise or not. Knowing what I know about how easy it is for me to lapse back into inactivity leaves me in no doubt about the fact that this is my Achilles heel. Any time the voice in my head says something like – "I haven't got time to exercise today" or "I'm too tired to go to the gym", I choose to remember how much progress I've made from the days when that voice would have stopped me from exercising completely, and how much better my body is feeling now that I'm building my fitness back up again. Maybe I am busy, so I do a shorter session. Maybe I am tired, so I do a restorative yoga session to reenergise my body. The important thing for me is not to continue to cave in and do nothing at all. That's a well-worn old pattern that I'm really committed to staying ahead of now.

I consider the mindset changes that I've made around exercise and a lot of other things I talk about in this book, to be the lynch pin in relation to my ability to maintain the lifestyle changes I've made since starting to include more Sirtfoods in my diet. I can't tell you how good it feels to be moving again. It goes back to what I was saying about mindset earlier. I might never get around to running a marathon, but that doesn't mean that I'm not benefitting from not short-changing myself in relation to my ability to push through discomfort, and trust my body to know how far to go, which by the way is invariably further than my mind thinks that it is.

My hope for you is that you're going to give yourself a chance to experience a sense of empowerment in relation to getting fit like I have. Wherever you are right now, you'll find that before too long you'll start looking better, feeling better, and ageing better if you find ways to put your body under the good physical stress that exercising to build muscle, flexibility and cardiovascular health involves. The fact is that our bodies are made to move. We can get away with inactivity when we're young, but sooner or later we'll start to notice changes in the way a body that isn't exercised feels and looks that we're not going to like. My hunch is that if you've been leading a sedentary life and the downside of that reality hasn't already hit home, then it is likely to hit home sometime in the not too distant future.

CONCLUSION

The mindset related exercises in this book will help you to work through whatever comes up that might be holding you back from claiming your right to wellness and achieving a healthy weight. By the end of this book or at least sometime shortly thereafter you'll be more likely to be eating well, relaxing more, and being kinder to yourself than you might have been for a very long time. You'll be well resourced to ease out of your old way of thinking and behaving, into a much more empowered and dynamic way of life. If it works as it should, the combination of things going on in this regard should prove to be greater than the sum of the parts, making it possible for you to align your behaviour around exercise and the other core areas of your life with your overall health goals.

If you start doing some, most, or all of the strategies around food, exercise, stress management, sleep and mastering your mindset that I've talked about in this book, before too long I would expect you to be much more comfortable about saying 'I am enough'. The exercises and other recommendations in this book are all about bringing your body into an optimal state to support the mindset changes you're working toward cultivating here and vice versa. Particularly important is sleeping well, stressing less, exercising regularly, eating well in general, and getting yourself off sugar in particular. As far as I'm concerned, sugar from sources other than fruit screws with our brain and disrupts our body in a way that I for one don't want any part of anymore. It is totally counterproductive to my efforts to stay well.

Make no mistake here, it doesn't make any difference at all how many books like this you read if you don't do anything to address shortcomings in your own life. If for whatever reasons you can't or simply don't get around to making any of the changes that you know will make your life in general and your weight in particular easier to live with, I urge you to contact me at wellnesscoachingcollective.com and I'll fill you in on the retreats and other programs I run that makes transformation much easier to achieve than it is when you go it alone.

I want to wish you well with all of my heart. You deserve to be well, and I want nothing less for you.

REFERENCES:

Cheat the Clock: How New Science Can Help You Look and Feel Younger, Pressler, Margaret Webb. (2012). New York. Alpha. A Member of the Penguin Group (USA) Inc.

Daring Greatly: How the Courage to be Vulnerable Transforms the Way We Live, Love, Parent and Lead, Brown, Brene. (2013). London. Penguin Books.

Mindset: The New Psychology of Success, Carol S. Dweck (2006). USA. Ballantine Books a division of Penguin Random House.

Nutrition Made Clear (audiobook), Anding, Roberta H. (2009). USA. The Teaching Company.

The Brain That Changes Itself: Stories of Personal Triumph from the Frontiers of Brain Science, Doidge, Norman. (2008). USA. Viking Penguin. A Member of the Penguin Group (USA) Inc.

The Complete Idiot's Guide to Menopause, Pelletier, Maureen Miller, and Romaine, Deborah S. (2000). Indianapolis. Alpha Books.

The Hero with a Thousand Faces (Third Edition with revisions). Campbell, Joseph (2008). USA. New World Library.

The 10 Secrets of Healthy Ageing. How to Live Longer, Look Younger, and Feel Great, Holford, Patrick and Burne, Jerome. (2012). New York. Hachette Book Group

The Sirt Food Diet Recipe Book, Goggins, Aidan and Matten, Glen. (2016). Great Britain. Yellow Kite, An imprint of Hodder & Stoughton.

The Willpower Instinct, McGonigal, Kelly. (2012). New York. Avery. A Member of the Penguin Group (USA) Inc.

The Wisdom of Menopause: Creating Physical and Emotional Health and Healing During the Change, Northrup, Christiane. (2001). USA. Random House Inc.

Thrive, Huffington, Arianna. (2014). UK. Penguin Random House.

Unleash the Power of the Female Brain, Amen, Daniel G. (2013). USA. Harmony Books.

Why Zebras Don't Get Ulcers, Sapolsky, Robert M. (2004). New York. McMillan Publishers.

Hierarchy of Needs: A Theory of Human Motivation, Abraham Maslow

ONLINE

ABC online: *www.abc.net.au/news/2013-11-22/australia-second-in-world-in-anti-depressant-prescriptions/5110084*

Anthony Robbins Training: *www.training.tonyrobbins.com/the-6-human-needs-why-we-do-what-we-do/*

Better Health: *www.betterhealth.vic.gov.au/bhcv2/bhcarticles.nsf/pages/Fibre_in_food?open*

Diabetes Australia: *www.diabetesaustralia.com.au/Understanding-Diabetes/Diabetes-in-Australia/*

Healthline: *www.healthline.com/health-blogs/hold-that-pause/35-symptoms-perimenopause*

Jean Hailes for Women's Health: *www.jeanhailes.org.au/health-a-z/menopause*

National Centre on Sleep Disorders Research: *www.nhlbi.nih.gov/about/org/ncsdr/*

National Sleep Foundation: *www.sleepfoundation.org*

Sleep Health Foundation
www.sleephealthfoundation.org.au/pdfs/news/Reawakening%20Australia.pdf

The Heart Foundation: *www.heartfoundation.org.au*

The Menopause Centre: *www.menopausecentre.com.au*

University of California San Francisco

www.ucsf.edu/news/2011/12/11091/stress-reduction-and-mindful-eating-curb-weight-gain-among-overweight-women

US Centres for Disease Control and Prevention: *www.cdc.gov*

ABOUT THE AUTHOR

As well as being a gifted speaker and author, Jane Turner is a sought after Transpersonal Coach with Master Coaching qualifications through the Behavioural Coaching Institute. Jane is also a Neuro Linguistic Programming  Master Practitioner, and holds Counselling for Health and Social Care qualifications through the Medical Register of Australia.

In addition to a range of wellness programs, Jane also runs a book writing program to fast track her clients to published author status.

Visit www.wellnesscoachingcollective.com.au and www.writewithjane.com to tap into the online resources Jane has made available to support you.

www.ingramcontent.com/pod-product-compliance
Lightning Source LLC
Chambersburg PA
CBHW072048290426
44110CB00014B/1594